THE

AUDACIOUS WAR

CLARENCE W. BARRON

1st WORLD
LIBRARY
Literary Society

The Audacious War

Clarence W. Barron

© 1st World Library, 2006
PO Box 2211
Fairfield, IA 52556
www.1stworldlibrary.com
First Edition

LCCN: 2007920629

Softcover ISBN: 978-1-4218-3939-4
Hardcover ISBN: 978-1-4218-3839-7
eBook ISBN: 978-1-4218-4039-0

Purchase *"The Audacious War"*
as a traditional bound book at:
www.1stWorldLibrary.com/purchase.asp?ISBN=978-1-4218-3939-4

1st World Library is a literary, educational organization
dedicated to:

- Creating a free internet library of downloadable ebooks

- Hosting writing competitions and offering book
  publishing scholarships.

Interested in more 1st World Library books?
contact: literacy@1stworldlibrary.com
Check us out at: www.1stworldlibrary.com

1st World Library Literary Society

Giving Back to the World

"If you want to work on the core problem, it's early school literacy."

- James Barksdale, former CEO of Netscape

"No skill is more crucial to the future of a child, or to a democratic and prosperous society, than literacy."

- Los Angeles Times

Literacy... means far more than learning how to read and write... The aim is to transmit... knowledge and promote social participation."

- UNESCO

"Literacy is not a luxury, it is a right and a responsibility. If our world is to meet the challenges of the twenty-first century we must harness the energy and creativity of all our citizens."

- President Bill Clinton

"Parents should be encouraged to read to their children, and teachers should be equipped with all available techniques for teaching literacy, so the varying needs and capacities of individual kids can be taken into account."

- Hugh Mackay

IF!

Suppose 't were done!
The lanyard pulled on every shotted gun;
Into the wheeling death-clutch sent
Each millioned armament,
To grapple there
On land, on sea and under, and in air!
Suppose at last 't were come—
Now, while each bourse and shop and mill is dumb
And arsenals and dockyards hum,—
Now all complete, supreme,
That vast, Satanic dream!—

Each field were trampled, soaked,
Each stream dyed, choked,
Each leaguered city and blockaded port
Made famine's sport;
The empty wave
Made reeling dreadnought's grave;
Cathedral, castle, gallery, smoking fell
'Neath bomb and shell;
In deathlike trance
Lay industry, finance;
Two thousand years'
Bequest, achievement, saving, disappears
In blood and tears,
In widowed woe
That slum and palace equal know,
In civilization's suicide,—

What served thereby, what satisfied?
For justice, freedom, right, what wrought?
Naught!—

Save, after the great cataclysm, perhap
On the world's shaken map
New lines, more near or far,
Binding to king or czar
In festering hate
Some newly vassaled state;
And passion, lust and pride made satiate;
And just a trace
Of lingering smile on Satan's face!
—*Boston News Bureau Poet.*

This poem has been called the great poem of the war. It was written just preceding the war, and published August 1 by the "Boston News Bureau." Of it, and its author, Bartholomew P. Griffin, the following was written by Rev. Francis G. Peabody: "The English poets, Bridges, Kipling, Austin, and Noyes, have all tried to meet the need and all have lamentably failed. I am proud not only that an American, but that a Harvard man, should have risen to the occasion."

CONTENTS

PREFACE

The Scotch have this proverb: "War brings poverty. Poverty brings peace. Peace brings prosperity. Prosperity brings pride. And pride brings war again." Shall the world settle down to the faith that there is no redemption from an everlasting round of pride, war, poverty, peace, prosperity, pride, and war again?

But it was not primarily to settle, or even study this problem that I crossed the ocean and the English Channel in winter. As a journalist publishing the *Wall Street Journal,* the *Boston News Bureau,* and the *Philadelphia News Bureau,* and directing news-gathering for the banking and financial communities, I deemed it my duty to ascertain at close hand the financial factors in this war, and the financial results therefrom.

I found myself on the other side, not only in the domain of the finance encircling this war, but unexpectedly in close touch with diplomatic and government circles. The whole of the war, its commercial causes, its financial and military forces, its tremendous human sacrifices, the conflicting principles of government, and the world-wide issues involved, all lay out in clear facts and figures after I had gathered by day and night from what appeared at first to be a tangled web.

I learned who made this war, and why at this time and for what purposes, present and prospective; and from facts that could not be set down categorically in papers of state. No papers, "white," "gray," or "yellow," could present a picture of the war in its inception and the reasons therefor.

There is no powerful organization over nations to keep the peace of Europe or of the world, as nations are in organization over states, and states over cities, to insure peace and justice, without strife or human sacrifice.

The immediate causes of this war, and I believe they have not before been presented on this side of the ocean, are connected with commercial treaties, protective tariffs, and financial progress.

It may be wondered that in our country, which is the home of the protective tariff system and boasts its great prosperity therefrom, there has been as yet no presentation of the business causes beneath this war. Our great journalists are trained to find interesting, picturesque, and saleable news features from big events. Details of war's atrocities and destructions are to most people of the greatest human interest, and rightly so. As a country we have no international policy, and European politics and policies have never interested us.

Germany is buttressed by tariffs and commercial treaties on every side. Years ago I was told in Europe that the commercial treaties wrested from France in 1871 were of more value to Germany than the billion dollars of indemnity she took as her price to quit Paris. But I did not realize until I was abroad this winter how European countries had warred by tariffs, and that Germany and Russia were preparing for a great clash at arms over the renewal of commercial and tariff treaties which expire within two years, and which had been forced by Germany upon Russia during the Japanese War.

German "Kultur" means German progress, commercially and financially. German progress is by tariffs and commercial treaties. Her armies, her arms, and her armaments, are to support this "Kultur" and this progress.

I believe I have told the story as it has never been told before. But the facts cannot be drawn forth and properly set in review without some presentation of the spirit of the peoples of the

Clarence W. Barron

European nations.

If all the nations of Europe were of one language, the spirit, the soul of each in its distinctive characteristics might stand out even more prominently than to-day.

Then we could see even more clearly the spirit of brotherhood and nationality that stands out resplendent as the soul of France. We should see the spirit of empire and of trade, interknit with administrative justice, as the soul of Great Britain. We should see Germany an uncouth giant in the center of Europe, viewing all about him with suspicion, and demanding to know why, as the youngest, sturdiest, best organized, and hardest working European nation, he is not entitled to overseas or world empire.

But few persons on this side have comprehended the relation of this great war to the greatest commercial prizes in the world; the shores of the Mediterranean, Asia Minor, with its Bagdad Railroad headed for the Persian Gulf, Mesopotamia with its great oil-fields, undeveloped and a source of power for the recreation of Palestine and all the lands between the Mediterranean, the Indian Ocean, and Asia.

The greatest study for Americans to-day is the spirit of nations as shown in this war, and great lessons for the United States may be found in the finance, business, patriotism, and justice that stand forth in the British Empire as never before. She is rolling up a tremendous war-power within her empire and throughout Europe, encircling the German war-power. But she is likewise looking to her own people and her own workers, filling her own factories and every laboring hand to the full that she may keep her business and profits at home, and with her business and profits and accumulated capital and income prosecute the greatest war of history.

She is not unmindful in any respect of what the war may send her way. In the breaking-away and the breaking-up of Turkey, she sees a clear field for Egypt, the realization of the dream of

Cecil Rhodes of the development of the whole of Africa by a Cape to Cairo Railroad, and she sees her own empire and peoples belting the world in power, usefulness, and justice, and with a sweep and scope for enterprise and development beyond all the previous dreams of this generation.

The United States, with hundreds of millions of banking reserves released and giving base for a business expansion double any we have had before, seems suddenly paralyzed in its business activities and, comprehending only that the loaf of bread is a cent higher and a pound of cotton a few cents lower, it is wondering on which side of its bread the butter is to fall.

Meanwhile, it talks politics, asks if prosperity here is to come during or after the war; and having little comprehension of the meaning of the national throbs that on the other side of the globe are pulsating the world into a new era of light, liberty, and expansion by individual labor, it refuses to take up its daily home-task and go forward.

In the hope that these pages may be useful to my fellow countrymen in giving them the facts of this war, its commercial causes, its financial progress, its sacrifice in humanity,—sacrifice that could not be demanded but for a greater future,—these papers are taken, as completed in my financial publications in this month of February, and placed before the reading community in book form, as requested in hundreds of personal letters.

They were never conceived or written with any idea of their permanent preservation. They were prepared for the banking community, which demands news-facts and figures discriminatingly presented. The banker wants the truth; he will make his own argument and reach his own conclusions.

The reader will readily see that these chapters are day-to-day issues aiming to present that news from the standpoint of finance. But under all sound finance must be primarily the truth of humanity. They do not claim to be from beginning to end a harmonious book-presentation of the war, but it is believed that they contain the essential fundamental war-facts; and the aim was to present them in most condensed expression.

They cover the first six months of this most Audacious War. Whether it is to continue for another six months or another sixteen months is not so material as the character of the peace and what is to follow.

No greater problem can be placed before the world than that of how the peace of nations may be maintained. Having cleared my own mind upon this subject, I submit it in the final chapter, which naturally follows after that treating of the lessons for the United States from this war.

Only in an international organization, with power to make decrees of peace and enforce them, and with insurance of powers above those of all dissenters, can we find the peace of nations as we have found the peace of cities. This Audacious War has forced such an alliance as can yield this power. Its transfer to the support of an International tribunal can make and keep the peace of Europe and eventually of the world.

Then may the earth cease to be, in history, that steady round of Prosperity, Pride, and War.

C. W. Barron.

February 15, 1915.

CHAPTER I

THE WORLD'S GREATEST CONTEST

The Censorship—The Warship "Audacious"—Mine or Torpedo?—The Battle Line—War by Gasolene Motors—The Boys from Canada—The Audacity of it.

The war of 1914 is not only the greatest war in history but the greatest in the political and economic sciences. Indeed, it is the greatest war of all the sciences, for it involves all the known sciences of earth, ocean, and the skies.

To get the military, the political, and especially the financial flavor of this war, to study its probable duration and its financial consequences, was the object of a trip to England and France from which the writer has recently returned.

One can hear "war news" from the time he leaves the American coast and begins to pick up the line of the British warships—England's far-flung battle line—until he returns to the dock, but thorough investigation would convince a trained news man that most of this war gossip is erroneous.

This war is so vast and wide, from causes so powerful and deep, and will be so far-reaching in its effects that no ill-considered or partial statements concerning it should be made by any responsible writer.

The difficulty of obtaining the exact facts by any ordinary methods is very great. There is a strict supervision of all news, and to insure that by news sources no "aid or comfort" is given to the enemy, a vast amount of pertinent, legitimate, and harmless news and data is necessarily suppressed. The censors are military men and not news men, and act from the standpoint that a million facts had better be suppressed than that a single report should be helpful to the enemy. Only in Russia are reports of news men from the firing line allowed.

One hears abroad continually of the battle of the Marne, of the battle of the Aisne, of the contest at Ypres, and the fight on the Yser, but no outside man has yet been permitted to describe any of these in detail, or to give the strategy, beginning, end, or boundaries of them, or even the distinct casualties therefrom. Indeed, it is doubtful if the official histories, when they are written, can do this, for these are the emphasized portions of one great and continuous battle that went on for more than one hundred days.

To illustrate the strength of the hand on the English war news, it may be noted that there is no mention permitted in the English press of such a ship as the "Audacious." Yet American papers with photographs of the "Audacious" as she sinks in the ocean are sold in London and on the Continent. Outside of London not ten per cent of the people know anything concerning this boat or her finish.

This word "finish" would be disputed in any newspaper or well-informed financial office in London where it is daily declared that although the "Audacious" met with an accident, her guns have been raised and will go aboard another ship of the same size, purchased, or just being finished, and named the "Audacious." Indeed, I was informed on "good authority" that the "Audacious" was afloat, had been towed into Birkenhead and that the repairs to her bottom were nearly finished. You can hear similar stories wherever the "accident" is discussed. I have heard it so many times that I ought to believe it. Yet if one hundred people separately and individually make assurances concerning something of which they have no personal knowledge, it does not go down with a true news man. I was able to run across a man who saw the affair of the "Audacious." He laughed at the stories of shallow water and raised guns. His position was such, both then and thereafter, that I was sure that he knew and told me the truth.

Later I learned that the "Audacious" was too far off the Irish coast to permit of talk of shallow water, and that neither guns nor 30,000-ton warships are raised from fifty-fathom depths.

Yet I am willing to narrate what has not been permitted publication in England, and I think not elsewhere: that the mines about Lough Swilly, along the Scotch and Irish coasts, and in the Irish Sea, were laid with the assistance of English fishing-boats flying the English flag. These boats had been captured by the Germans and impressed into this work.

There are also stories of Irish boats and Norwegian trawlers in this work, but I secured no confirmation of such reports.

It is still unsettled in British Admiralty circles as to whether the "Audacious" came in contact with a mine or torpedo from a German submarine. Two of her crew report that they saw the wake of a torpedo. Reports that the periscope of a submarine showed above the water I have reason to reject.

English reports were suppressed—the admiralty claimed this right, since there was no loss of life—in the belief that if the ship was torpedoed by a submarine, the Germans would give out the first report, and thereby be of assistance in determining the cause. But to-day the Germans have their doubt as to where the "Audacious" is, and as to whether or not she was ever really sunk.

Expert opinion is divided in authoritative circles in England as to the cause of the disaster; but more than 400 mines have been swept up along the Irish and Scotch coasts by the English mine sweepers.

While upon this subject, I ought to narrate that the study of this topic has convinced me that the Germans have a long task if they hope within a reasonable number of months to reduce by submarine torpedo practice the efficiency of the English navy to a basis that will warrant German warships coming forth to battle.

Every battleship is protected by four destroyers. Submarines, when detected, are the most easily destroyed craft. They have no protection against even a well-directed rifle bullet. Their whole protection is that of invisibility. Their plan of operation is to reach a position during the night, whence in the early morning they can single out an unprotected warship or cruiser not in motion, and launch against her side a well-directed torpedo, before being discovered.

The place for England's battleships is where they are: in the harbors with their protecting nets down until they are called for in battle. In motion or action, submarines have little show against them.

The Japanese at Port Arthur found that protecting nets picked up many torpedoes and submarines. Since that time, torpedoes have been made with cutting heads to pierce steel nets encircling the warships, but their effectiveness has not so far been practically demonstrated.

It is Kitchener's idea to keep the enemy guessing. Therefore he was rather pleased than otherwise when the story of Russians coming through England from Archangel was told all over the world. The War Office winked at the story and certainly had no objection to the Germans getting a good dose of it. I think that story might have been helpful at the time when the Allies were at their weakest, but they do not now need Russians, or stories of Russians, from Archangel.

The story must also go by the board that a submarine north of Ireland meant either a new type of boat that could go so far from Germany, or an unknown base nearer Scotland.

Submarines as now built could go from Germany around the British Isles and then across the Atlantic—in fair weather.

The eastern boundary of France divides itself into four very nearly equal sections. Italy and Switzerland are the lower quarters of this boundary line; and of the upper quarters Belgium is the larger and Germany the smaller. The southern half of the German quarter boundary is a mountain range and on the open sections stand the great fortifications of France and Germany, regarded by both countries as practically impregnable. The defence of France on the Belgian frontier was the treaty which guaranteed the neutrality of the smaller country.

When Germany's conquering hosts came through Belgium, the war soon became a battle of human beings rather than of fortifications. Neither the French nor the Germans had learned from practical experience the modern art of fighting human legions in ground trenches, but both sides quickly betook themselves to this rabbit method of warfare.

To-day from Switzerland to the North Sea is a double wall of 4,000,000 men, all fighting, not only for their own existence but for the existence of their nationality—their national ideals. They are protected by aeroplanes, flying above, that keep watch of any large movements.

They are backed by 4,000,000 men in reserve and training who keep the trenches filled with fighting men, as 10,000 to 20,000 daily retire to mother earth, to the hospitals, or to the camps of the imprisoned. On the North Sea and the English Channel they are supported by fleets of battleships, cruisers, submarines, and torpedo boat destroyers that occasionally "scrap" with each other, the German boats now and then attacking the English coast and harbors and the English boats now and then assisting to mow down the German troops when they approach too near the coast. But the great dread and key to this naval warfare is the modern submarine.

Submarines, aeroplanes, and motor busses are three elements of warfare never before put to the test; and the greatest of these thus far is the gasolene motor-car. By this alone Germany may be defeated. France and England are rich in gasolene motor power, and supplies from America are open to them. A year ago there were less than 90,000 motor-cars in Germany, and Prince Henry started to encourage motoring to remedy this, but the Germans are slow to respond in sport. Indeed they know little of sport as the English understand it, of sportsman ethics or the sense of fair play in either sport or war. They do not comprehend the English applause for the captain of the "Emden" and stand aghast at the idea that he would be received as a hero in England. When a daring aeroplane flier in the performance of his duty has met with mishap and, landed on German soil, he is not welcomed as a hero. He is struck and kicked.

The German is not to be blamed. It is the way he has been educated to "assert himself," as the Germans phrase it. Indeed, when the captain of the "Emden" was taken prisoner and was congratulated by the Australian commander for his gallant defense, he was so taken aback that he had to walk away and think it over. He returned to thank his adversary for his complimentary remarks. With true German scientific instinct he had to find his defeat in a physical cause, remarking, "It was fortunate for you that your first shot took away my speaking tubes."

The English are sports in war,—too sporty in fact. General Joffre warned General French over and over again, "Your officers are too audacious; you will soon have none to command," and his words proved true. The English officers felt that the rules of the game called upon them to lead their men. They became targets for the guns of the foe, until one of the present embarrassments in England is the unprecedented loss of officers.

This has now been changed and Kitchener insists that both officers and men shall regard themselves as property of the

Empire, that the exposure of a single life to unnecessary hazard is a breach of discipline. For this reason Victoria Crosses are not numerous, less than two dozen having been conferred thus far; and it has been quietly announced that no Victoria Crosses will be conferred for single acts of bravery or where only one life is involved. It must be team work and results affecting many.

For this reason also it has been decreed that the 33,000 Canadians in training at Salisbury Plain shall not be put in the front until they have learned discipline in place of the American initiative.

These Canadian boys receive their home pay of four shillings, or $1 per day, while the English Tommy gets one quarter of this amount. The Canadians are fine fellows, feeling their independence and anxious to be on the firing line, but the War Office recognizes that soldierly independence cannot be allowed in this war. It is not improbable that the Canadian troops will eventually be dispersed that their strong individual initiative may be thoroughly harnessed under the organization before they are trusted in the trenches. They are not to be permitted to go there to be shot at, but to use their splendid physiques, fighting abilities, and patriotism—more British than the English themselves—in strict organization.

This is not to be an audacious war on the part of the Allies. It is first a defensive war in which the Germans are the heaviest losers. On the part of the Germans it is an audacious war and its very audacity has astounded the whole world. But Germany never meant to war against the world collectively. That was the accident of her bad diplomacy.

The audaciousness of Prussian war conceptions began in the latter part of the last century. They did not grow out of the war with the French in 1870, for Bismarck's legacy to the German nation was a warning against any war with Russia. The German scheme was concocted by the successor of Bismarck himself, none other than Kaiser William II. He planned a steady growth of German power that would first vanquish the Slav of southeastern Europe and give Germany control through Constantinople and Asia Minor to the Persian gulf; then, as opportunity arose, a crushing of France and repression of Russia; and the overthrow of the British empire; and then the end of the Monroe Doctrine, to be followed by American tariffs dictated from Germany.

This seems so audacious a program as to be almost beyond comprehension in America. Yet it will be made clear in the next chapter.

CHAPTER II

TARIFFS AND COMMERCE THE WAR CAUSES

War with Russia was Inevitable—Finance and Tariffs made Germany great—Commercial War—How Germany loses in the United States—The Tariff Danger.

For the causes of this most audacious war of 1914 one must study, not only Germany and her imperial policy, but most particularly her relations with Russia. These relations are very little understood in America, but they become vital to us when open to public view.

Disregarding all the counsels of Bismarck and the previous reigning Hohenzollerns, the present Kaiser has steadily offended Russia. War with her within two years was inevitable, irrespective of any causes in relation to Servia. Russia knew this and was diligently preparing for it. Germany—the war party of Germany—knew it and with supreme audacity determined through Austria first to smash Servia and put the Balkan States and Turkey in alignment with herself for this coming war with Russia.

Sergius Witte is one of the great statesmen of Russia. He formulated the programme for the Siberian railroad and Russian Asiatic development. The party of nobles opposed to him arranged that he should receive the humiliation of an ignoble peace with Japan, under which it was expected that

Russia would have to pay a huge indemnity.

But when Witte arrived at the naval station at Portsmouth, New Hampshire, to make the famous treaty with Japan, his first declaration was, "Not one kopeck for indemnity." He won out and returned in triumph to Russia.

But during the progress of the Japanese war Germany thrust her commercial treaties upon St. Petersburg. Goods from Russia into Germany were taxed while German goods went under favorable terms into Russia, with the result that Russia has had a struggle now for ten years to keep her gold basis and her financial exchanges.

It was Witte who was sent to Berlin to protest against these proposed treaties and secure more favorable terms. Witte made his protest and refused to accept the German demands. Then suddenly he received peremptory orders from the Czar to grant all the demands of Germany. The Czar declared Russia was in no condition to have trouble with Germany. These commercial treaties expire within two years. Russia many months back proposed the discussion of new terms. Germany responded that the present treaties were satisfactory to her and he should call for their renewal.

This meant either further humiliation to Russia or war. Russia had already suffered the affront of being forced by Germany at the point of the bayonet to assent to the taking by Austria of Bosnia and Herzegovina in violation of the Treaty of Berlin. The Czar realized many months ago that Russia must now fight for her commercial life. She would not, however, be ready for the war until 1916.

Let Americans consider what this means—a German war over commercial tariffs—and see what, if successful in Europe, it would lead to.

The German nation is a fighting unit under the dominion of Prussia, the greatest war state, not only of the empire, but of the world. Having welded Germany by the Franco-Prussian war into a nation with unified tariffs, transportation, currency, and monetary systems, Prussia has been able to point to the war as the cause of the phenomenal prosperity of Germany.

It is a popular fallacy in Germany that militarism makes the greatness of a nation. Germany's prosperity did not begin with the war of 1870. This was only the beginning of German unity which made possible unified transportation and later unified finances and tariffs. Several years after the war, France, which had paid an indemnity to Germany of a thousand million dollars, or five billion francs, was found, to the astonishment of Bismarck, more prosperous than Germany which had thus received the expenses of her military campaign and a dot of Spandau Tower war-reserve moneys.

In 1875 came the great Reichsbank Act, which consolidated all the banking power of the empire. Then came her scientific tariffs which put up the bars here, and let them down there, according as Germany needed export or import trade in any quarter of the earth. The German people, on a soil poorer than that of France, worked hard and long hours for small wages. But they worked scientifically and under the most intelligent protective tariff the world has ever seen. In a generation they built up a foreign trade surpassing that of the United States and reaching $4,500,000,000 per annum. By her rate of progress she was on the way to distance England, whose ports and business were open to her merchants without even the full English income tax. She built the biggest passenger steamers ever conceived of and reached for the freight carrying trade of the world. She mined in coal and iron and built solidly of brick and stone. She put the world under tribute to her cheap and scientific chemistry. She dug from great depths the only potash mines in the world and from half this potash she fertilized her soil until it laughed with abundant harvests.

The other half she sold outside so that her own potash stood her free and a profit besides. No nation ever recorded the progress that Germany made after the inauguration of her bank act and her scientific tariffs. The government permitted no waste of labor, no disorganization of industry. Capital and labor could each combine, but there must be no prolonged strikes, no waste, no loss; they must work harmoniously together and for the upbuilding of the empire.

Germany did not want war except as means to an end. She wanted the fruits of her industry. She wanted her people, her trade, and her commerce to expand over the surface of the earth, but to be still German and to bring home the fruit of German industry.

Germany has been at war—commercial war—with the whole world now for a generation, and in this warfare she has triumphed. Her enterprise, her industry, and her merchants have spread themselves over the surface of the earth to a degree little realized until her diplomacy again slipped and the present war followed—such a war as was planned for by nobody and not expected even by herself. She was giving long credits and dominating the trade of South America. She had given free trade England a fright by the stamp, "Made in Germany." She was pushing forward through Poland into Russia to the extent that her merchants dominated Warsaw and were spreading out even over the Siberian railroad. Her finance was intertwined with that of London and Paris.

In the United States she was the greatest loser. Here taxes were lowest and freedom greatest. German blood flowed in the veins of 20,000,000 Americans and not one fourth of them could she call her own. The biggest newspaper publisher in America, William Randolph Hearst, figured that New York was one of the big German cities of the world. He turned his giant presses to capture the German sentiment. He spent tens of thousands of dollars upon German cable news, devoting at times a whole page to cable presentations from Europe which he thought would interest Germans. But the investment proved fruitless; he found there was in America no German sentiment such as he had reckoned upon. He could not increase his circulation, for the German-Americans seemed little concerned as to what

Clarence W. Barron

happened in Berlin or Bavaria.

Prussia learned what Hearst learned, that Germans were soon lost in the United States. She studied this exodus and the wage question and by various arts and organizations arrested the German emigration to America. She saw to it that employment at home was more stable. It was figured that if the German emigration could be centralized under the German eagle it would be to her advantage. The question was where to get land that could be made German. Europe has for some years expected a German dash in Patagonia, and the Europeans outside of Germany have taken very kindly of late years to the Monroe Doctrine. In Africa and the islands of the sea the German colonial policy has not been a success. Dr. Dernburg as colonial secretary has many a time stood up in the Reichstag and warned the Germans that the home military system and rules were not adaptable to colonization in foreign parts; that Germans must adapt themselves to foreign countries and not attempt at first to make their manners the standard in the colonies they undertook to dominate.

While German colonies have not yet passed beyond the experimental stage, German tariffs and German commerce have been great successes.

The population of Russia is 166,000,000 people. This is the latest figure I gathered from those intimate with the government at St. Petersburg. This is just 100,000,000 more than Germany. Germany thinks she must trade to her own advantage with the people now crowding her eastern border.

The example of America in putting up tariff bars against "Made in Germany" has many advocates in England and in the rest of the world.

When France, only a few years ago, was angered that Italy should sign up in "triple alliance" with Austria and Germany, she did not dare to attack Italy with arms, but she did attack Italy by tariff measures, and for a time Italy and France fought—by tariffs.

What might be the position of Germany if the American protective tariff system were expanded over the earth? In the view of some people tariffs, taxation, and armaments go hand in hand. There is a town in Prussia that finished payment only twenty years ago on the indemnity Napoleon exacted from it.

Can a country afford to develop an industrial system dependent upon an outside world and then suddenly find the outside world closed by tariff barriers?

When an American ambassador protested against Bismarck's discriminatory treatment of American pork, the great chancellor asked, "What have you to talk with? You have no army or navy." "No," said the American ambassador, "but we have the ability to build them as big as anybody. Do you wish to tempt us?" "No," said the German chancellor, "and your goods shall not be discriminated against."

Dr. Dernburg has given the key to the German colonial military, tariff, and financial policy. German unity in tariffs and transportation has made German prosperity, and Dr. Dernburg, her former colonial secretary and now in New York, says the mouth of the Rhine and the channel ports must be free to Germany and that Belgium must come into tariff and transportation union with Germany. Belgium is being taxed, tariffed, pounded, and impounded into the German empire.

There is some difference in size between Belgium and Russia, but no difference in principle with respect to their German relations.

"World power or downfall," Bernhardi put it.

Clarence W. Barron

CHAPTER III

THE POLITICAL CAUSES OF THE WAR

A State with no Morals—A Peace Treaty sundered—Where Germany fails—A Thunderbolt.

Sending his little expedition to China the Kaiser said:—

"When you encounter the enemy you will defeat him; no quarter shall be given, no prisoners shall be taken. Let all who fall into your hands be at your mercy. Just as the Huns one thousand years ago, under the leadership of Attila, gained a reputation in virtue of which they still live in historical tradition, so may the name of Germany become known in such a manner in China that no Chinaman will ever again dare to look askance at a German."

Belgium was made an example of. According to the German idea she should have accepted money and not stood in the way of German progress.

German military progress is allied with German commercial progress. It is a mistake in the conception of Germany to imagine that she wars for the purpose of war or for the development and training of her men.

The first principle of German "Kultur" as respects the state is that the sole business of the government is to advance the interests of the state. No laws having been formulated in respect to the business of a state, the government is without moral responsibility, and the laws applicable to individual action do not apply to the state. Individuals may do wrong, but the state cannot do wrong. Individuals may steal and be punished therefor, but the state cannot steal. It is its business to expand and to appropriate. Individuals may murder and be punished for the crime, but it is the business of the state to kill for state development or progress.

The English-speaking conception of morality is that what applies to an individual in a community applies to the aggregate of the individuals, that the state is only the aggregate of the individuals exercising the natural human functions of government for law and order.

This is entirely outside the German conception. In the German conception a government comes down from above and not up from the people. It is not the people who rule or govern, but the government from above rules the people, and the people must implicitly follow and obey; thus is national progress and human progress. The whole of Germany believes in the government of the Kaiser: that law and war flow down through him and that neither can be questioned by the individual. Obedience, union, efficiency, progress, and progress through war, if necessary, are cardinal virtues.

Germany does not desire war with Russia, but German progress requires the continuance of present tariff relations, and if war is a means to that desirable end, war is divine.

The murder of the Crown Prince of Austria was an incident furnishing Germany and Austria opportunity to carry out their long-conceived programme for the extension of their influence through the growing state of Servia.

A treaty had been arranged between Greece and Turkey, and was to have been signed in July, which would have settled many things in respect to Turkey and the Balkan states.

Clarence W. Barron

Roumania and Servia were in agreement concerning this great measure for peace in southeastern Europe.

When all was ready for the final conference and the signatures, Austria intervened and announced her opposition. Then suddenly followed the bombshell of the ultimatum to Servia, timed at the precise moment to stop the signing of this Turkish treaty.

Austrian officials admitted privately as follows, and I have it directly from parties to the negotiations:—

"We are satisfied that Servia would punish the murderers of Prince Ferdinand if we so requested. We are satisfied she would apologize to Austria if we requested it. But our aims go beyond. We demand that instead of the proposed Turkish treaty the Balkan states shall come into union with Turkey under the influence of Austria. To accomplish this we must accept no apology, but must punish Servia. We are satisfied that Russia is in no financial or military position to interfere."

Germany with its enormous spy system had secured copies of the confidential state papers of the Czar and transmitted them to Vienna. In these were warnings, statistics, and compilations showing all the financial and military weaknesses of Russia: that her great gold reserve had been largely loaned out and was not available cash on hand, as the world had been led to believe; that it would take eighteen months more of preparation to place her military forces in position to defend the country; that her arms and the factories to build them were not ready.

The plans of Austria and Germany were to line up the Balkan states, under German political and trade influences, and then within two years to have it out with Russia and again impose the German tariffs upon her. If France dared to come in, it would certainly be an attack, and Italy would, under the Triple Alliance, assist to defend Austria and Germany. Defeating Russia, Germany could, at that time or later, crush France in the manner in which Bismarck had said she might eventually be crushed by Germany for Germany's progress.

Then, having made more onerous tariff treaties with France than were exacted from her in 1870 and having extended German trade and military influence over Russia, Germany would be in a position with her navy to try out the long desired issue with Great Britain for the control of the seas.

Admiral Von Tirpitz told the emperor that it must be at least two years more before the German navy would be able to try conclusions with England.

The German plan was to take the European countries one at a time. The German information was that every country except Germany was unprepared, and that information was true. She was fully prepared except in her navy.

One of the leaders among those great business Lords of England, who sit with the Commoners in business, but in the House of Lords as respects legislation, said to me when I spoke of the wonderful intelligence of Germany in research and data, scientific and political: "But, don't you think that the Germans had too much information and too little judgment?"

In other words, they had a stomach full of facts but no capacity todigest them. They knew as much about Ulster and perhaps more than London as respects facts and detailed information, but they were in no position to pass judgment upon Ulster or the unity of the British Empire the moment there was an attack from the outside. The Germans have dealt in materialistic facts. But with the spirit that moulds and makes history they are all awry. With the Germans, individuals are units and are counted from the outside, never from the inside. That is why her diplomacy is not only a failure, but offensive: it never differentiates among nations and peoples according to that which is within the mind and the heart of the people.

The German Emperor directed the Austrian ultimatum to

Clarence W. Barron

Servia, insisting upon stronger demands than were at first proposed. Then, turning his back upon the scene, he was able to protest that he was not responsible. Yet the published correspondence from every capital in Europe now shows that the German Emperor fenced off every attempt to get Austria to modify or postpone or discuss her demands. Germany was ready for everything except the interference of Great Britain.

A private telephone rang at five o'clock one morning in Berlin and an American lady was informed from a social quarter that "Something dreadful has happened." "Something awful—something undreamed of." The American lady quickly asked, "Has the Kaiser been assassinated?" as the tone over the telephone indicated nothing less.

The response was, "England has declared war!"

That was the most unlooked-for step in all the German calculations.

Every spy report, every diplomatic agency, military and civil, had reported that England was out of the running: Ireland in revolution, India in sedition, Canada, Australia, and South Africa just ready to break away from the British yoke.

The conception of the British empire as a federation of free peoples governing themselves, under a constitutional monarchy, is something incomprehensible in the German idea of government. The German idea is of colonies attached to and paying tribute to the crown, something to be ruled over, governed, taxed, and made to serve.

Russia might go to war exposing in the field her weakness already spread out on paper by Russian authorities, with copies in Vienna and Berlin; but that England or Great Britain could or would fight at this time was an impossibility; although later England was to become "The vassal of Germany."

And the wonderment of Germany has become the

wonderment of the world. "Roll up," said Kitchener, and 2,000,000 men sprang to arms. More than 800,000 of them are on the Continent; 1,700,000 of them are in training.

"Roll up," said Lloyd George, the Chancellor of the British Exchequer; and $1,700,000,000 of war loan is rolling into the British Treasury, a sum one half the national debt of England and nearly twice the national debt of the United States.

If necessary, the number of men in arms will be doubled to 4,000,000 and the enormous subscription just made to England's war loan will be doubled and quadrupled.

The life of the empire as respects money and men is at stake, and no sacrifice is too great. If treaties are "scraps of paper" and neutral states are to have no rights or protection, there is no safety in the world, no sacredness of contracts; the world is at an end and chaos reigns.

Clarence W. Barron

CHAPTER IV

PEACE PROPOSALS

The Bagdad Railroad—The English Oil Concession—The German Alliance with Turkey—Austria the Hand of Germany —The Decay of Turkey—The New Map.

How ridiculous are American peace proposals concerning the Audacious War of 1914 may be judged from this announcement which I am able to make:—

The return of the French government from Bordeaux to Paris was determined upon from two points of view: safety and political necessity. The French people were angered that Paris should have been deserted, but notwithstanding the political reasons, which were more forceful than the public will be permitted to know, the return would not have been undertaken had not the military authorities considered the move a safe one. How safe will be evidenced by this—that at both Bordeaux and Paris this problem was before the authorities: "Events have now progressed so far that it is time for the Allies to consider what will be their terms of peace. These terms must be divided into many classes, ranging from those in which only one of the Allies has an interest to those in which all have an interest. Of course, the latter will be the most complex, and it is time now to begin with the complexities of the most far-reaching situation. This is Mesopotamia and the Bagdad railroad."

Now who in Washington knows anything about Mesopotamia or the Bagdad railroad? Yet here is the key of the most far-reaching problem in any peace proposals. It is because this matter can now be settled that the plunging of Turkey into the war by Enver Bey has made all Europe rejoice. The Germans think Turkey is another 16 1/2-inch howitzer or "Jack Johnson" putting black smoke over the British empire. The rest of Europe now knows the whole of Turkey is on the table, and the carving, it is believed, will be had with no plates extended from either Austria or Germany. For the first time the Turkish problem can be really settled instead of patched.

Some years ago I was astonished to learn in Europe that American banking interests, and American contracting and engineering firms in alliance therewith, had their eyes upon Asia Minor and the possibility of its development by American railroad enterprise. I was astonished to learn that some people at Constantinople had authority for the use of the name of J. P. Morgan & Co. Indeed, a railroad concession in Asia Minor, the details of which it is not now necessary to go into, had been arranged, I was told, and lacked only signatures. The American people felt that the Germans were the little devils under the table who stayed the hand of the Sultan, and kept his pen off the parchment. Never would the signature come down on that paper, although declared to have been many times promised.

The English were, of course, vitally interested in any railroad concessions in Asia Minor as opening the route to the Persian Gulf and India. Money talks with Turkey as nowhere else. The Germans had made a great impression upon the Bosphorus. Nobody at that point in the geography of the world could fail to see the wonderful commercial progress of the Germans and the military power that stood behind ready to back it up.

A concession for a railroad from the Bosphorus to Bagdad and through Mesopotamia to the Persian Gulf finally went to Germany, and the signature of the Sultan was at the bottom of the paper. There was, of course, the usual Oriental

Clarence W. Barron

compromise, and the concession for the oil fields of Mesopotamia went to the English; but the signature of the Sultan is still lacking to that piece of paper.

English statesmen announced that the Bagdad railroad was a purely private enterprise, financed in Germany by people associated with the Deutsche Bank. They had later to confess that error. Germany laughed and later openly announced that the Bagdad railroad was a Prussian enterprise of state. In fact, this concession, which is likely to be famous in history when the Allies win, was handed over to the German Emperor personally by the Sultan.

Already a thousand miles of this road have been constructed through Asia Minor to Mosul. The concession carries the mineral rights for ten miles on either side of the railroad, except through the oil fields of Mesopotamia, said to be among the greatest of the oil fields of the world. They are really part of the famous Russian oil territory between Batum and Baku, or the Black and Caspian seas, which extends not only south into Mesopotamia but is now being developed far to the north in the Ural Mountains of Great Russia.

Steadily the influence of Germany progressed with Turkey, now through one channel, now through another. When the Bulgarian war broke out, it was German guns and German officers and German money that upheld the Turks. The French put their money on Bulgaria by bank loans to her treasury. The Russians backed Servia. The French laughed and so did all Europe when the Turkish troops manned by German officers were beaten back to Constantinople and the Bosphorus.

Austria extended the hand of friendship to Bulgaria and induced her to attack her allies, Servia and Greece, thus making the second Balkan war. The result was the loss by Bulgaria of part of the territory she had acquired and a further augmentation in the importance of Servia. Bulgaria has never forgiven either Servia or Austria for this defeat.

The Servians are the pure-blooded Slavs, while the Bulgarians have a Turkish admixture, whence their great fighting qualities. The Roumanians just north of Bulgaria are Italians, and the defeat of Turkey in Africa by Italy did not lessen the importance of this enterprising nation on the Danube, fronting Austria-Hungary and Russia. Both Austria and Germany were losers in all three wars; while the treaty ending the second Balkan war magnified Servia of the Slav race of Russia. This is the important and crucial point in race and geography.

Austria, as the hand of Germany, still demanded a union of all these Balkan states with Turkey and under the aegis of Austria,—which meant, of course, Germany.

The aim of Germany in alliance with Turkey was, through Austria in *quasi*-sovereignty over the Balkan states, to carry German influence by the Bagdad railroad right through Asia Minor to the Persian Gulf. Germany would thus be, when the work was finished, a mighty military empire with rail communications cleaving the center of Europe and extending through Asia Minor to Eastern waters. With her growing steamship lines she would touch her colonies in the Pacific and her mighty naval base at Kiao-Chau in the Far East.

Now, while Germany is besieged on all sides and Italy and Roumania are preparing to go into the war with the Allies that they may have their part and parcel in the settlements, it is recognized that it is none too early for the Allies to consider the map of the entire eastern hemisphere and tackle that most difficult problem, the Bagdad railroad, from which Turkey, Asia Minor, Mesopotamia, and Palestine, the great historic countries of the world, must be parcelled out or dominated and developed.

The followers of Mohammed are no longer a unit. They number 175,000,000 people in the aggregate, but India and Egypt have gradually receded in sentiment from decadent Turkey, now numbering only about 20,000,000 people, and defended by an army of about 1,000,000. But this is no longer an army of united, fighting Mohammedan Turks; only a mixed army lacking in unity, discipline, efficiency and financial base.

Indeed, such are the financial straits of Turkey that a ten per cent tax has been levied upon the property of the people. If you hold property in Turkey and cannot pay ten per cent of the value the authorities have assessed against it, it may be sold or confiscated for the tax.

Where the money goes, nobody knows. German influence with Turkey has a financial base; 6,000,000 pounds sterling or 100,000,000 marks went from Germany to Constantinople just before the war, according to reports I have from people in the international exchange markets. From diplomatic sources I learn that this was just one half of the payment made by Germany to Turkey. The other 100,000,000 marks was probably paid in war supplies, including the two famous German warships that the English allowed to escape from the Mediterranean into Turkish waters.

The little English boy was right who returned from school the other day and said, "Hurray! I don't have to study any more geography; the old maps are to be torn up and the new map has not yet been made."

It is because of the making of this new map that European diplomacy is rolling on underneath the surface faster than ever before. Bulgaria has demanded as the price of her neutrality that she shall have what she lost in the second Balkan war. The Allies have responded: "What you get must depend upon what Servia gets from Austria and in the carving up of Albania." Austria-Hungary may lose Bosnia, Herzegovina, Dalmatia, and some more. So far as Servia acquires territory here Bulgaria may push farther south, recovering Adrianople and more sea coast on the Aegean.

Roumania wants Transylvania just north in Hungary,

occupied by 2,500,000 people, the majority Roumanians—this will make her 10,000,000 people—and Italy wants territory from Austria and naval ports on the Adriatic sea.

Neither Italy nor Roumania has its full war supplies and equipments. Servia, however, has been terribly pounded by Austria and but for her good fortune in pushing Austria back out of Servia in December, the Roumanians with their 450,000 well-organized troops might have had to come to her assistance earlier than was prepared for. Indeed, it is now expected that Italy and Roumania will move against Austria within a few weeks. Russia and the Allies are making their agreements for this intervention.

And what does America know about these movements on the European chessboard, and upon what basis should she aspire to be arbiter or peace adviser?

CHAPTER V

FRANCE AND THE FRENCH

Signs of War not Conspicuous—Paris reopened—A Rejuvenation—English and American Help—French Casualties—French Heroes.

One enters France nowadays by the Folkestone and Dieppe route, which is a four-hour Channel trip or longer, or by Folkestone and Boulogne, a Channel trip of ninety minutes more or less. All the routes to Calais are used by the government for its troops, supplies, and munitions. England's hospital base is at Boulogne. Here is the center of her Red Cross work, with a dozen big hospital ships commandeered from the P. & O. line and bearing distinctive stripes around their hulls. One hospital ship is set apart for the wounded Indians, and the apartments within are fitted up according to the various religious castes prevalent among the troops of India now fighting in France and Flanders. Here at times puts in Lord Zetland's yacht, fitted out by Queen Alexandra for wounded English officers.

When you travel by rail, if you did not know that war was in the country you would never suspect it, unless you wondered why a red-hatted, blue-coated guard, with a rifle carelessly swung over his shoulder, is noticeable now and then by a cross-road or near the buttress of an important railroad bridge. You pass trains of troops, but the uniforms are quiet, the men jovial and unwarlike. The wounded are not conspicuously moved by day.

Although you are not many miles away from the firing line, where an average of more than ten thousand are daily falling, the country is as peaceful and quiet as can be imagined. The big black and white horses are winter ploughing. The red and black cattle and the sheep and hogs are grazing in fields and pastures. The reddening willows speak of an early spring, and the full blue streams tell the brown grasses, and the tall poplars that their colors will soon be gayer.

As the shadows fall, no guard comes as in England to pull your curtain down according to military orders; and, as you approach Paris, you see families dining by uncurtained windows in blazing light. You are astonished after your London experience of semi-darkness to find the boulevards ablaze and no apparent fear of aerial enemies or sky-invasion, although aeroplanes and Zeppelins and bombs may be flying and fighting only eighty miles away. Now and then a searchlight illumines the heavens, but even searchlights are far less conspicuous than in London. In January the lights were ordered to be lowered; but Paris will not stand for long London fog, gloom, or darkness. The French atmosphere and life demand light.

Paris is gradually getting accustomed to the situation. More than 30 first-class hotels are partially opened and advertising. Many of the business streets have a semi-Sunday appearance. Boulevards running from the Place de l'Opera are well filled with people, and nearly all of the stores are now open. In the first weeks of December you could see the reopening day by day, and when on the 10th the government returned to Paris, the art stores and the jewelry stores joined with the confectioners, trunk dealers, and book-men, and threw open shutters that had been closed four months.

Paris is now normal but not crowded. Theaters are reopening, but the restaurants must be closed at ten P.M. The inhabitants young and old picnic in the Bois de Boulogne and evince most interest in the defences about the Paris gates,—the moats, the new trenches that have been dug, and the tree-trunks that have been thrown down with their branches and tops pointing outward as though to interrupt the progress of an enemy. Buildings have been taken down, and the forts of Paris stand forth as never before; but when you learn how unmanned and how useless they are in modern warfare, you can but smile and join with the people in their curiosity excursions. A single modern shell can put a modern stone-and-steel fort, garrison and guns, entirely out of commission.

A year ago Paris looked dirty and decadent. Her building fronts were grimy, her streets were dirty, and there was a general carelessness where before had been art, precision, and cleanliness. To-day Paris streets are clean. There is even more evidence of rebuilding and of modern conveniences. Motor street-sweepers whirl through the squares, not singly but in pairs and more extended series, and they move with automobile rapidity, quickly cleansing the pavement.

I was reminded thereby of a personal experience at the breaking out of the Spanish-American War. At breakfast on a Sunday morning with one of America's most successful millionaires, I said, "How is it possible that the stock market can be rising as the country is going to war—a war that may cause some of our new warships to turn turtle and may bring bombardment upon our sea-coast cities? Yet before the guns are booming the stock market is booming. Indeed, the stock market began to boom from the time we declared a state of war."

And this successful multi-millionaire replied quietly, "Stocks are going up because I am buying them and every other intelligent capitalist is buying them. Look out of the window there. That sweeper at the crossing has straightened up and is sweeping that crossing better and with more energy because the flags are flying, and the bells are ringing, and the guns will soon be booming. War is the greatest energizer of a people.

There is now profit in industry and enterprise, and financial equities have increased value." And for nearly ten years the stock market booms followed in the wake of that war boom, while construction and upbuilding went steadily forward despite agitation and restricting laws.

It would astonish Mr. Wilson and Mr. Bryan to know how many patriotic Americans are helping France and what they are doing in Red Cross and other work. I was surprised to meet a former member of the New York Stock Exchange in a khaki uniform. I said, "Are you still an American citizen?" He responded promptly, "Certainly I am, but would not the boys on the floor of the Exchange be astonished to see me in this uniform?"

I said, "Were there not men enough here to do this work?"

He responded, "Possibly, but quick organization was wanted, and I volunteered and have held the job." And he was off in his high-powered automobile for a run down behind the firing line to one of the Channel ports.

As the casualties of the French have been ten times those of the English, American and English sympathizers have turned to France to see if they might "do something." An English lady with small feet and delicate hands responded to the spirit of the hour, left her English home and her servants, and went to the hospital front in France. She wrote home: "I am helping not only to dress the wounds, but to wash dishes. My soft hands are parboiled but hardening; my feet are sore; and my legs are swollen. I lie down thoroughly exhausted every night, but I am doing something and am happy."

Mrs. W. L. Wyllie, wife of the famous marine etcher on the south English coast, looked out upon the Channel war-scenes, and took ship for France. She found the center and south of the country one vast hospital. At Limoges alone she found more than 12,000 wounded, and 32,000 wounded had passed through that city. She found the hospital in need of special bandages and cross-bandages for multiple wounds, and back she flew to England for bales of bandages. For weeks she was crossing and recrossing the English Channel. Soldiers have recovered from as many as twenty and thirty bullet-wounds in the flesh.

An American lady assisting in the English Red Cross work told me that she saw 2000 wounded every day for eleven days arriving at Boulogne. About the middle of December I learned that orders had been given to clear the Boulogne hospital base and prepare for a large number of wounded. Relief days for the troops at the front were shortened, and it was intimated to me in good quarters that the Germans would enjoy no Christmas in their trenches. The Allies advanced, counted their dead and wounded, and ceased in the attack.

I do not believe that any great forward movement can be made on either side from or against these trenches in the winter time. In good strategy and diplomacy, the break-up of Germany should come from other quarters.

There is considerable typhoid arising from the trench-work, but I heard it stated in medical circles that the Servian troops, with their milder climate, had found a new way of healing wounds. Not having the hospital base and equipment of other countries, they heal their wounds in the open air with the result that there is no tetanus or lock-jaw. In Switzerland human tuberculosis is now being cured by exposing the chest, directly over the affection, to the full rays of the sun.

The casualties of this war have been tremendous for France. No lists of her dead or wounded are published; it was at first a life-and-death struggle. While the total casualties—killed, wounded, missing, and prisoners—were estimated in the press reports and by the people as 600,000, I happen to know that they were more than 1,000,000. Of these, of course, one third or more will return to the battle-line, and the French have the satisfaction of knowing that the German losses are far larger. But, viewed from a financial standpoint, if this war is not too prolonged or too costly in life and treasure, France will emerge from it rejuvenated and reenergized.

Her people are serious and determined as never before. They now welcome strong work and strong hands, and if the Republic does not respond to the responsibilities of the hour, they will not as in 1870 burn and destroy, but will set up another government in quick order and wipe out the weakness and inefficiency found to exist when the strain came in August, 1914.

The French nation has never before been put to such a trial. In every other war there has been no threat of the destruction of France. Indeed, up to 1870 France was the great nation of Europe, greatest in war as well as greatest in peace. When she attacked Germany in 1870, she started for Berlin with full confidence in her greatness. And when she paid to the Germans a billion dollars in 1871, it was with scorn and contempt: "Take your money and get out!"

When Bismarck in 1875 discovered the prosperity of France, he cunningly set about encompassing her downfall. He knew the world would not approve of Germany attacking a foreign foe; there was no excuse that could be found.

Therefore, as he himself has confessed, he started France into empire-colonial upbuilding in Africa and Asia, with the full intention of leading her into a clash with England. When this point was reached many years afterwards, Delcasse clearly saw the situation, and, instead of war, made friends with England. All the world knows the result. Germany demanded his resignation from the French Cabinet under threat of war. France was humiliated, Delcasse dropped. Later he led the movement to strengthen the navy of France as well as the army. It may be declared that Delcasse created the Triple Entente and thereby saved France and Europe. To-day France fights a wholly defensive battle, supported on the one side by the Russian bear and on the other by the British lion. And strongest in the new cabinet of France stands Delcasse.

France was chastened by the war of 1870. She will be crushed or redeemed by the war of 1915. The spirit of her people to-day is the spirit of sacrifice. The French character never before shone forth so nobly.

"What a terrible disfigurement!" exclaimed a thoughtless lady as she visited the wounded in a great French hospital.

"Not a disfigurement at all, madame," exclaimed the French soldier. "A decoration!"

Out of this war may come great political and military heroes. There is one general in France to-day whose name is not widely known but of whom his associates say, "He is not only the equal but the superior of Napoleon." But the great hero throughout Europe to-day is the King of the Belgians, of that little country that grew daily bigger in the eyes of the world as it grew daily smaller in possessed territory. There are those who believe that France and Belgium will be hereafter closer together than before, and that—stranger things have happened —the King of the little Belgians might be no greater miracle for France than the little Corsican more than one hundred years ago.

CHAPTER VI

THE POSITION OF FRANCE

The Iron Hand of War—Paris offered in Sacrifice—Faulty Mobilization—The French Army—The Joffre Strategy—The German Retreat.

The position of France to-day cannot be compared with that of any other country in the war. The French people have a distinctive genius all their own. They are still the greatest people in art in the world. Nothing in sculpture or painting in the outside world yet rivals the skill of France. Politically the French are trusting children, vibrating between empires and republics, and following only the rule of success. In finance they were accounted great a generation ago. In savings they have been regarded as world-leaders.

When the stern reality of military necessity suddenly confronted France five months ago, there was the same old story of graft, fraud, and a deceived people.

But the war authorities gripped France with an iron hand. The military traitors and grafters are in jail. The weaklings in the official line have been cashiered. The politically undesirable have been given foreign missions.

There was political as well as military wisdom in the return of the government from Bordeaux to Paris. The French people

Clarence W. Barron

were shocked when they learned that the boasted military defences of Paris, "the most extensive fortifications in the world," embracing 400 square miles, were unprovisioned and indefensible, that the government had fled, and that there was no army to save the city.

Indeed, the authorities had determined to sacrifice Paris to save France. General Joffre had no men to spare to be bottled up in the city. He determined that his armies should be kept free on the field.

You may ask anywhere in France, Belgium, or England why the French did not come to the relief of Belgium, why Paris was undefended, and what saved it after Von Kluck had led seven armies of 1,000,000 men down to its very gates, and you will get no satisfactory answer.

But when you have studied the situation and the record, you will see that no simple answer can be readily given. A brief one would be: French mobilization plans were imperfect, and, therefore, Belgium could not be defended by the French. But motor-busses did what the railroads were unprepared to do, and finally saved Paris and France.

The French had been warned many months publicly and privately that their mobilization plans would be found faulty in case of sudden hostilities. The railways moved perishable goods at the rate of thirty miles a day while German and Austrian railways bore military trains at the rate of thirty miles an hour.

So ill prepared were the French in their mobilization plans that they actually summoned to arms the men who were to man the railways, and the railways themselves were deficient in rolling-stock to move the troops. The citizens responded promptly enough, but France had no bureaucracy or military plans to match those of Germany, and, as throughout French history, the leaders of the people failed at the crucial moment. The plodding English had to help out the French railway plans, and then had to turn around and find their own railroad defects. When England first sounded the call to arms, men deserted the railroad service to go into training to such an extent that the authorities had to stop it and maintain transportation as, of course, an important arm of the war-service.

The history of the unpreparedness of both England and France has yet to be written. It would not be useful to print much that is already known. There are two political sentiments in both countries, and political issues will rise again in both after the war.

A little contemplation here will show the extravagance of many estimates of the number of men to be put in the field in time of war. Many estimates have taken little account of the number of men required to handle a modern transportation service, and the supply organization to back up an effective army at the front. Transportation and war-supplies are on such an expanded basis as was not dreamed of a few years ago. The war plans of one generation cannot be the war plans of another either on land or sea. That France had 4,500,000 men capable of bearing arms did not mean that she could hold 4,000,000 men in fighting array at any one time.

After five months of war France had only 1,500,000 men at the front, and from the camps and military organizations she expects to have ready a fresh army of another million in the spring. But she mobilized nearly 4,000,000 men. Paris industry, trade, and commerce could shut down in a day, but there was no organization that could make in a day or a week the men of France into an army at the front. Her 600,000 regular troops were, of course, always in position to be thrown on the defensive at the German frontier. None of the nearly 4,000,000 additional men could be got with arms and munitions of war into Belgium, to meet effectively the trained troops of Germany.

The German troops were "moving" as early as July 25, while all the governments of Europe, including Austria, were negotiating for and hopeful of peace. When war was declared against France, she promptly offered Belgium five French army corps for defence. King Albert declined, saying there had been no invasion of Belgium by Germany, and that Belgian neutrality was guaranteed by treaty. Within two days the German guns were firing on Belgium; but when King Albert then called upon France for protection, the response was that the French troops which had been offered had been placed elsewhere. The regular troops probably had. The new troops were not mobilized, and the French transportation system, to say the least, had not been as responsive as expected.

France paid dearly for her unpreparedness. Her richest provinces were invaded by the Germans and are still held by the Germans in considerable part.

Caught unprepared, there was only one safe thing for General Joffre to do—let the Germans expand far from their base while the French concentrated between the German border and Paris, to strike back at the opportune moment against an extended and weakened line.

The march of the armies of Von Kluck—"General One O'clock," they called him, and said his fiercest attacks were at one o'clock—is considered a masterpiece of military precision. The strategy of General Joffre which foiled him is praised throughout France.

The plan of the Germans was to hold the north of France with the army of Von Kluck while the Crown Prince moved from Luxemburg straight to Paris. This was theatrical, dramatic, and Kaiserlike; but the French would not consent. They persisted in holding Verdun and defeating the armies of the Crown Prince.

The English are the greatest fighters in the world in retreat, while the French can fight best in a forward movement. The little expeditionary army of England, originally 100,000 men but at this time 180,000 men, held the right flank of Von

Kluck in the retreat from river to river, from hill to hill, although pounded by 350,000 trained German troops massed on this flank. This retreat put the stamp of English bravery and dogged determination, as before, on the map of Europe. Paris was open and exposed to any entry which the Germans wished to make. The government had retired, the gold reserves of the banks had been moved, the people in large numbers had fled.

Indeed, I may say what has never before been printed, that President Poincare summoned the "architect" of the city to the American embassy and, with tears streaming down his face, told him whence he must take his orders in the future.

Then in a flash went the orders of Joffre along his whole concentrated line of troops: "The retreat has ended, not another foot; you die here or the enemy goes back!" He had chosen the psychological moment. The French and English had burned and broken the bridges as they retreated, and with the recoil the German communications were in danger.

A fresh force of 50,000 held in reserve near Paris flew by motors and motor-busses against the right wing of Von Kluck, which the English in retiring had been punishing so heavily. Von Kluck had been drawn too far into France with no support on his left from the army of the Crown Prince, which the French had held at bay but with a tremendous sacrifice of men. The German ammunition and supply-trains were broken and the armies of Von Kluck were hurled back from Paris about as rapidly as they had come forward.

Then the Kaiser took a hand and cried, "Now for the English; take the Channel ports; forward against Calais!" and again, as at Liege, the blood of the Germans soaked the soil of Belgium. The Allies dug themselves into the ground behind the rivers and canals, and drowned the Germans out in front; and when an advance by the seacoast was attempted, the English naval guns spilled havoc into the German battalions. Four nationalities grappled in a death-struggle, but the wall of the Allies held from Switzerland to the sea. The Allies worked most harmoniously. Belgian knowledge of topography proved superior to the German general-staff maps. The English buttressed the French financially and in transportation and food-supplies. Indeed, Kitchener at one time fed two French army corps, or 80,000 troops, for eleven days without a hitch.

Although England had not the trained men, she had the fundamentalmilitary organization, transportation, food, and finance.

CHAPTER VII

FRENCH FINANCE

Delayed Budgets—The Caillaux Position—Outgeneralled in Finance—Gold Reserves Undiminished—Allied Finance—No Financial Legislation—The National Defense Loans.

The spectacle of England loaning money to rich France— 20,000,000 pounds sterling, or $100,000,000—was something most surprising.

The French have been considered among the best financiers and economists of Europe. The whole world has been envious of the saving ability of France, and has invited the overflow of her accumulations into their local enterprises. For many years France has had the lowest interest rates and a considerable surplus to invest in outside countries. It is upon France that Russia has mainly relied for funds for her expanding industrial development. In the Baring crisis she sent her gold to London to fortify the situation, and in the American crisis of 1907 she extended her hand across the sea. Then she turned about and steadily built up her gold reserve in the Bank of France, from $500,000,000 to above $800,000,000, although her people were not expanding in population, industry, or enterprise. France had grown so confident that she seemed at one time to have lost her financial cunning.

In Germany in 1913 I was told that German finance had

passed through the "fire test," that two years of building recession and of expanding commerce had placed her on a solid financial base; and it was true.

I was told to step over to Paris and see a disordered budget, an increasing national deficit, bad investments in Mexico and South America, and disorganized finance. I did and found it all true. I also found that France was fully able to take care of herself without any outside help, and, but for the specter of outside interference, to delay her financing if she so elected.

It has been something of a mystery as to how there could be two Balkan wars and so little of public finance behind them. Of course, Russia and France helped the Balkan States and Germany helped Turkey. The money of France came from the French banks and was loaned to the treasuries of the Balkan States and to Greece—to Bulgaria 350,000,000 francs; to Greece 250,000,000.

The French government said that this could not be financed by public issue after the war until the national budget itself had been arranged, although French bankers were permitted to float a $50,000,000 Servian loan. With the increasing cost of labor and supplies the French railways had been steadily running behind, and France had to face a deficit in her budget of something like 1,000,000,000 francs, or $200,000,000, per annum.

It was proposed last January that the government should consolidate its indebtedness and put its financial house in order, by an issue of long-term securities; but Caillaux opposed the programme and defeated it for many months. This postponed the issue of the Balkan States' loans.

To-day Caillaux is about the most hated man in France. Although he is financially well-to-do, the people believe that his connections and sympathy with Germany were too close. The German press took his side in the famous Calmette shooting affair and the trial of Madame Caillaux, and all this record now stands forth most threateningly in the French blood.

I may perhaps be permitted to say that M. Caillaux has been under arrest, and that the police of Paris have declared they would not be responsible for his safety. It has, therefore, been diplomatically arranged by the government that he should be now in Brazil upon a semi-diplomatic and trade mission.

The French loan just before the war was not a popular success. The reason is now obvious. It was sold short from other European capitals where it was better known that war was in the air.

When a famous "bear" operator reappeared upon the Paris Bourse after his return from Vienna, whence he had conducted his attack on the French loan, he was greeted with a storm of hisses. The French Bourse is a government institution and must support the credit of France and her allies. In Vienna they knew war was planned for the end of September, even before the assassination of the Austrian Crown Prince at Serajevo June 28. This event hastened but did not make the war.

Nevertheless, instead of permitting the French banks to bring out the Balkan loans thereafter, the French authorities allowed Turkey to come into the French market with a loan for 25,000,000 pounds, or 625,000,000 francs.

Some people pleaded with them that this money would be used against France, and that every franc would go to repay the German loans; and they were right.

In this financial situation France was suddenly plunged into war, and while Germany and England have been raising money by the billion, the marvelous thing is that France has made no public issue beyond one-year notes, but continues to pay her bills in gold and has the exchanges all in her favor. Money is flowing in, and not out.

Clarence W. Barron

It was most marvelous to find in France, in the fifth month of the war, prompt payment, no distrust of the government paper issues, gold and paper circulating side by side, and no strain for gold as in Germany.

Nevertheless, the war has been fought thus far for the most part on the paper issues of the Bank of France and with the gold reserve of that bank undiminished.

This is most remarkable.

The first reason I can assign for it is that the French soldier gets twenty-five centimes, or five cents a day, or one fifth the pay of an English soldier. Kitchener's army is to-day costing far more than the entire French army. French food is locally abundant and cheap, notwithstanding the *octroi*, or French local tax of one eighth. The main need of the French from the outside is boots and horses. The English in France are not taxing French resources at all. All their food-supplies, including the hay for their horses, come from England.

The English troops are also well supplied with money from home. Outside the regular Tommy Atkins, the volunteers and territorials coming into France have abundant money. They are the men from the cities and from the wealthiest families in the country life of England. There are more than 300,000 of them on French soil, and as they come and go in France, they are spending not less than four shillings a day each, or nearly four times their wages. This makes a daily expenditure of 60,000 pounds sterling in France, and calling for exchange. Hence the English pound has been at the lowest price in France on record, 24.95 and sometimes 24.90.

There is also the additional reason of higher insurance rates for the transportation of money across the Channel,—a channel infested with mines and submarines. It is no uncommon thing for boats crossing the Channel to sight floating mines, and the wonder is that disasters therefrom have been so few.

The third reason is that France has very large investments and credit resources outside, and can still summon money from abroad.

You see more English than French soldiers in the life of Paris. Their khaki uniforms are as conspicuous there as in London.

The character of the early enlistments for the front in London is illustrated by the following story. An officer entered a restaurant where a group of English soldiers in khaki uniforms were enjoying their cigarettes and pipes. The officer threw some shillings on the table and called, "Waiter, give these men some beer."

And a khaki uniform snapped forth a sovereign on the same table, and cried, "Waiter, give this officer some champagne."

Bank statements are queer contraptions nowadays. While the United States, with less gold in the country and less reserve in the banks than formerly, is showing the most enormous surplus—and a legitimate and better-protected surplus by reason of the new bank act—and the Bank of England is counting $100,000,000 of gold in Canada as a London bank reserve, and Russia has counted, as gold in her reserve, money on deposit which has been loaned out on time; while Belgium is doing a banking business from an English base, and Germany is inviting gold from the jewelry of her inhabitants and boasting her gold strength, the Bank of France refuses to publish any statement, makes no boast, but holds more gold than ever before in her history.

Only a few weeks before the war was her metal base put above $800,000,000. Then she suspended official statements until one was made to the government December 10, and this showed $880,000,000 metal base, or 4,500,000,000 francs. Upon this her note issue, which was formerly 5,800,000,000 has been expanded to nearly 10,000,000,000. She is authorized to issue up to 12,000,000,000 francs in paper.

From this metallic base she increased her bills receivable by 3,000,000,000 francs, or about the same amount that the Bank of England discounted in pre-moratorium bills under the backing of the government. Each country took on $600,000,000 of mercantile credits, and both countries are now finding this item receding. In France the mercantile credits have been considerably reduced—the increase reduced nearly a half—because the men are at the front and business is not calling for the credits formerly in use.

The Bank of France also promptly advanced 8,000,000,000 francs or $400,000,000 to the government.

In the last few weeks of 1914 the finances of Russia, France, and Belgium became interlaced with those of England, and gold credits for the Allies' supplies were established around the world, shipments from North America going both east and west into the European war. Government credit with the Bank of France was then extended, but should not early in January have been more than $800,000,000.

This is the main financial assistance on which France for five months conducted a successful defensive warfare, with 1,500,000 men at the front and nearly 3,000,000 men behind them.

The next most remarkable financial feature in respect to France is that there has been no special financial legislation, in fact no financial legislation whatsoever, except the December budget vote to cover government expenses, including the war. A moratorium was set up by decree, but authorization for this already existed under the general laws. Under this moratorium payments were permitted at first of 5 per cent, then 25 per cent. Later depositors were permitted to draw from the banks 40 per cent, and 40 per cent payments became the rule. Then 50 per cent for December, and in January, 1915, full payment to bank-depositors, although legally the moratorium stands to March 1, 1915.

Among other temporary devices in French finance was the issue by French chambers of commerce in the south of France of small pieces of paper,—as low as 50 centimes or 10 cents,—used only for circulation and change locally.

Many banks closed their branches because they had not the clerks to man them. Many bankers lost three fourths of their staff when the mobilization orders were issued, and all over Paris the banks are closed from twelve to two because of the limitations of the staff. When the Credit Lyonnais reopened its branch in the Champs Elysees a few weeks ago it was manned by women clerks.

The government loan issued in the summer of 1914 met less than half of the floating indebtedness and 1914 ordinary deficit. The balance as maturing has been merged into the national-defense loan, which is only short-term financing. On the 10th of December there were 1,000,000,000 francs of the new national-defense loan outstanding, but it was being subscribed for all over France daily. This national-defense loan consists of three, six, nine, and twelve months' government bills bearing 5 per cent interest. I figured that the amount issued December 10 was for the most part used to provide for the maturing floating indebtedness, and for the deficit on the government budget aside from the expense of the present war.

As the government is advancing money to Servia and to Belgium, the loan of 20,000,000 pounds, or $100,000,000, from England can be readily accounted for.

There were loans from the big banks of France for the government at the opening of the war, but these loans I was assured were all merged in the 5 per cent national-defense loans, which have not exceeding one year to run.

On these national-defense loans the cautious Bank of France will advance in limited amounts 80 per cent of the face value, but only where the government loan matures within three months.

The great principle of the Bank of France is to keep liquid. Its assets must always be mobile.

There is only one point at which French finance should be criticized, and as we cannot know all the details of the stress of the military position when Paris was abandoned, her mobilizing of the reserves still in disorganization, and her transportation awry, we may not be in a position to level any just criticism.

But it must be set down in the interest of true report that the French credit was at one time endangered by the way the treasury, or the military authorities, handled the government credit in payment for war-supplies.

Instead of going to the bankers and making its financial arrangements, paying the war-supply contractors, the French government made many contracts under which it paid contractors, and purveyors, with the 6 per cent national-defense notes of the government, running three, six, nine, and twelve months.

As the contractors were making 15 per cent and 20 per cent on their mercantile overturn, they could afford to discount 5 per cent and more in the sale of the government notes, and while the government was passing out these notes at par to the patriotic subscribers, the contractors were negotiating liberal discounts to bankers and others.

Nevertheless, the stupendous fact remains that France, caught in a European war most unaware, with impaired budget and a floating indebtedness, has carried the greatest war of her history for six months without a long-term national loan and by the issue of less than $200,000,000 5 per cent short-term notes for not exceeding one year, and credits for less than $800,000,000 from the Bank of France; has maintained her gold basis unimpaired; and has kept the international exchanges steadily in her favor; and all this without any special financial legislation.

Nor could I find any evidence of a French disposition to sell the American copper shares, railroad bonds, or industrial shares into which the French have been putting some money of late years. But I did learn that short-term American railroad notes may this year be renewed abroad only in part.

CHAPTER VIII

THE BELGIAN SACRIFICE

No Migration from Belgium—Germany's War Tax Levies—
Irreconcilable—The Army—No Neutrality over Belgium.

Before Germany launched her thunderbolts of war, Belgium
had an industrious, frugal, hard-working, saving population of
nearly 8,000,000 people. Of these, 450,000 are now refugees
in Holland, where the magnanimous Dutch are providing for
them with no outside assistance. Queen Wilhelmina declares,
"These are our guests and we will care for them." Nearly
30,000 Belgian troops have also been interned in Holland. It
was expected that they might leak out, but the Dutch are stern
in their present position of neutrality. They understand their
very existence depends upon it. Some of the interned warriors
attempted to escape, and six were shot by the Dutch. Nor will
they permit contraband articles of war to go through their
country. While the Dutch may sell their own supplies as they
please, all imports of rubber, copper, or petroleum must be
accounted for, and their reexport to Germany is forbidden.

Germany also holds 30,000 Belgian soldiers as prisoners.
England took 18,000 severely wounded Belgian soldiers into
her hospitals, and 80,000 refugees are being there cared for
largely by private enterprise. The losses by the war are difficult
of estimation. But at the present time there are 7,000,000
people in Belgium, most of whom must be fed by the

outside world.

Belgium is the one nation from which the people have never migrated. Beyond war there is only one power that can move the Belgians from their soil, and that is the influence of the Church.

Representatives of American railroad and industrial interests are in Europe endeavoring to induce emigration from Belgium to the United States, but it is doubtful if these efforts will meet with any success. There are in the United States to-day only two Belgian settlements, one of about 1000 people in Montana and one of about 1500 in western New York. The Belgian loves his land and sits by his home though it be in ruins. The history of the land of the Belgians shows that, as the cockpit of Europe, it was the battle-ground of centuries; yet her people are more immobile than those of any other country in Europe. Earthquakes do not make sunny Italy or golden California less attractive to their inhabitants.

About $20,000,000 (more than 10 per cent of this came from Belgian people) has been raised to feed starving Belgians, and $20,000,000 more should be forthcoming.

The English war office objected at first to the American proposals for food supplies to the little country. It was held to be the duty of the invading Germans to feed the population of the conquered country, as the Germans had appropriated large stores of supplies that were in Belgium, notably at Antwerp.

England finally assented to the proposal, as well she might, for Belgium would starve without food from the outside, irrespective of war losses. In normal times, she imports 240,000 tons of food every month. She also imports most of her raw supplies for manufacturing. Belgium is, therefore, to-day without food, or raw materials for her industries, and probably without outlet had her industries the ability to produce. Although about fifty ships are bringing food to Belgium, they are of small capacity and in the aggregate represent less than one month's supply. In the early part of December about 80,000 tons of food were going through the American committee by permission of Germany and England. The people have been put on one-third rations. Every inhabitant of Belgium is allowed a pint of soup a day and about as much coarse brown bread as would make one American loaf.

The German idea of responsibility and power is that of force. They have ordered the people of Belgium to love them, cooeperate with them, and go about their business. But the Belgians refuse to love the Germans, refuse to cooeperate with them and will not resume their work for the Germans to appropriate the results. The people of Antwerp were invited to come back from Holland and it was proclaimed that there would be no indemnity levied, yet a huge one came down upon the city. The Germans levied a war tax of 50,000,000 francs on Brussels, and Rothschild and Solvay are not permitted to leave the city.

Payment on the tax was agreed to, and then the Germans demanded 500,000,000 francs from the entire province of Brabant, which includes Louvain as well as Brussels. The inhabitants said it was impossible and the demand was reduced to 375,000,000 francs. The inference must be that the latter levy covers a term of years.

The Germans are provoked that the bank money got out of Belgium. The Bank of Belgium sent its gold reserve to the Bank of England, 600,000,000 francs, and Germany demanded that this reserve be transferred from England to a neutral country; but, of course, England refused. There are some banks still doing business in Belgium, but the Belgians reject the German money except when obliged to take it.

The Belgian stores remain closed for the major part, and the Germans threaten that unless the Belgians reopen and proceed with business they will confiscate the stores and sell them to Germans who will do business. The people of Antwerp must be in bed by 9 o'clock. The people of Liege are ordered to retire at 7 P.M. No Belgian is permitted the use of a telephone, the entire system having been appropriated by the military authorities.

The Germans have decreed German time, which is one hour different from that of London, but the Belgian people refuse to set over their watches and clocks. The Belgian railroad system is different from that of the Germans,—left-handed tracks and a different system of signalling. The Belgians refuse to do the bidding of the Germans and operate the railroads. The Germans must move the trains themselves.

The Germans do not hate the Belgians. They simply pity them, that they were so shortsighted as not to accept German gold for right of passage through the country. The German hate is reserved entirely for the English above all people on the surface of the globe. In Belgium 200 marks reward is offered for the capture of any Englishman found in that domain.

The latest response to Bernhardi's book, "England the Vassal of Germany," is Kipling's poem in the King Albert book issued December 16 to augment the Belgian Relief Fund. I clip two verses:—

> They traded with the careless earth,
> And good return it gave;
> They plotted by their neighbor's hearth
> The means to make him slave.

> When all was readied to their hand
> They loosed their hidden sword
> And utterly laid waste a land
> Their oath was pledged to guard.

After the German Kaiser sounded the battle sentiment of Europe by sending the warship "Panther" to Agadir three years ago in violation of the treaty of Algeciras, it was intimated by the French and the English that Belgian neutrality might be in

Clarence W. Barron

danger; also that the Lord and the Allies helped those who help themselves.

Therefore, a bill was introduced in Belgium's Capital providing for the raising of an army of 600,000 men where before were 46,000 and a war footing of 147,000. The leader of the Catholic party opposed the programme, declaring that Belgian neutrality was guaranteed by Germany, France, and England. A compromise was effected by which an army of less than half this number was authorized.

When on Sunday evening, August 2d, at 7 P.M., the German ultimatum was handed to Belgium, she was given twelve hours or until morning to declare whether or not the country would be surrendered to the free passage of the German war battalions. Belgium had then an army of 200,000 men; 60,000 volunteers sprang to arms, and that 260,000 was the maximum Belgian army that attempted to withstand the millions of Germany's armed forces. Even these were not effectively placed. The 30,000 men at the frontier were not sufficient to permit of any effective sorties to protect the approaches to the Liege fortifications. It was a forlorn hope from a military standpoint, but for three weeks the Belgians with shrinking forces held in check the war power of Germany. Every week help was expected from the Allies, but no help came, for no country in Europe outside of Germany and Austria had any expectation of war.

Down to the ground and their graves fought the plucky little Belgians, until they numbered, not 260,000, but nearer 60,000. After every able-bodied man in Belgium was demanded by King Albert, the ranks of the Belgians began to swell, and, with able-bodied refugees returned from England, there are now about 120,000 men in the ten divisions of the Belgian army.

But England carries, as she ought, the financial burden. She feeds, clothes, and equips the Belgians and furnishes the money-supply. The Germans still strive, not so much against the Allies as against the English in Belgium. Here the fighting is fiercest, casualties are greatest, and here the reinforcements on both sides are the greatest per mile of line.

Meanwhile the more than a million Germans in Belgium have trenched across the whole country, rebuilt the forts at Namur, Liege, Antwerp, and other places, and are digging themselves into the ground doggedly and determinedly, and with as great precision and more science than the Allies. The German trenches are rather better made and the machinery for trenching has been, of course, better prepared by the Germans.

The great surprise of the war was the demonstration in Belgium that forts costing millions, in defense of cities, are absolutely useless against the big German shells. The defense at Liege was prolonged because the Germans could not at first find the exact location of the central defense. Finally a German approached bearing a large white flag of truce. Belgian orders were given to receive him. The German, under his flag of truce, signalled the desired information and then fell. Soon after, fell the fort. The Germans had found the desired range, and shot. At Antwerp a single shell was able to put an entire fortress out of business.

It is the Landwehr and the older men that have been called by Germany to do duty in Belgium, while the younger troops are sent back and forth between the eastern and western frontier defences.

An American who has lately been all through Belgium, representing both commercial interests and charity work, tells me;—

"I left America absolutely neutral. I was not a student of the war or of the cause of the war. What I saw in Belgium convinced me that the Allies must win and will win. I am no longer neutral. What I saw in Belgium of the wanton destruction of villages, towns, and cities has prejudiced me as no argument could have done. The Allies' losses will begin when they take the offensive against the German works which are now being constructed. Soon England will have 600,000 more men on the Continent and there will be more doing.

"The losses of the Germans have been two or three times the losses of the Allies in the Belgian trenches, because the Germans have been the attacking parties. If the Allies become the attacking parties they will have to sustain the heavy losses. But I cannot see it otherwise than that the Allies must win. The crime against Belgium is the greatest crime since Calvary, and it has set the whole world against Germany.

"It is not only a crime, but it was a military error, for to-day Germany has 600 miles of front to defend, 300 east and 300 west, and her losses have been enormous. At Liege 7000 Germans went down in a single day's fighting. One man I met assisted to bury 500 Germans in front of a single trench.

"I do not believe Brussels is mined; but if ever the Germans got into Paris they would destroy the whole city before they left.

"I shudder to think what the Germans will suffer at the hands of the Belgians when once the rout of the Germans has been begun by the Allies. The Belgians are unreconciled, and if they ever get weapons in their hands—well, I will not predict, I will just tell you one fact: I traveled the length and breadth of the land, saw the women and the children sitting by their ruined hearthstones, but I never saw a tear on the cheek of a Belgian."

CHAPTER IX

RUSSIA AND THE RUSSIANS

Russian Reforms—A United Russia—Russian Armaments—
The Greatest Future—Two Water Outlets—The Slav Invasion
Bugaboo.

Russia also is likely to bring forth some notable men who have
not previously been heard of before the world. General Evanoff
is the idol of the Russian army. He is the strategist who plans
the movements against Austria and Germany in the East, who
surrounds Przemysl and says, "Now, we can take it when we
please, but we will not sacrifice Russian troops to take it now;
Cracow is more important. Lodz is not important from a
military standpoint. We will surround it later."

Evanoff orders his men to keep out of the valleys and engage
the Germans in the open plain, where their own numbers will
count in action; for in the valleys the German big guns have
the advantage.

Russia has been at work steadily since the Japanese war
reforming her army within and without. More than one third
of her officers were dismissed after that war. The Russian
officials now say that the Japanese war was to Russia most
providential. It showed the lines of Russian weakness,
inefficiency, and graft, which could flourish at a distance from
St. Petersburg but became exposed when war put the Russian

organization to the test. Steadily every year Russia has been systematically and thoroughly routing out graft and inefficiency. When Russia starts to do a thing she does it thoroughly.

It was because Russia was rebuilding, reorganizing, and was indulging in criticism and putting its mind on the weak spots, that Russian confidential papers stolen in the interest of Germany misled both Berlin and Vienna as to the possibility of Russia going to war to defend Servia in the year 1914.

War has united Russia as never before. The Czar now moves about unattended, and the country is a unit behind him and the war and unitedly against the Germans. From Warsaw to Siberia the German agents and merchants have been arrested and impounded. Nobody in Germany can yet realize how this war has destroyed her commercial relations and commercial organizations throughout the world. Everywhere German people are subjects of suspicion. You will even hear in all seriousness that the Kaiser had an army of 150,000 reservists in the United States with a partial equipment of arms ready to attack Canada; and I have been told by supply agencies that these arms are now offered for sale, as the uselessness of any German movement on the American continent is apparent.

How far Germany is unable to measure the spirit of the English-speaking people is shown by the fact that she cannot understand why the United States does not take this opportunity to possess Canada.

I heard of a retired German-American of wealth, residing in Germany, who was actually invited to go to America to stir up a raid on Canada. Of course he obediently returned to the United States, and then he sat down to wonder how he could effectively report back the foolishness of such an idea without offense to Berlin.

Russia has been perfecting her military organization for ten years. The expansion was to come in the next two years. At the opening of the war she had only 2,500,000 available troops. For two years she has been building factories to manufacture ammunition and arms, and these are now being rushed to completion. People who have offered her contracts for arms and munitions have been told that Russian factories shortly to be completed will make their weapons more quickly than they can now be ordered and received from other countries.

With arms and equipment Russia can draw 17,000,000 men to her German-Austrian frontier just as readily as Germany can draw 7,000,000 men to both her frontiers. In both calculations only one in ten of the population is counted upon for service.

The story is told of a Russian who was asked in London why he did not return for military duty. He replied, "Oh, I belong to the 14th million, and it will be some time before the 18th million is called out."

Russia has the greatest future of any country in Europe. She has the largest unturned arable soil of any country in the world. Russia in Europe is a great agricultural plain. To the east are her rich oil-fields steadily expanding north in the Ural Mountains, and east lies Siberia, endowed by nature as one of the richest countries in the world, an area in which you could deposit the United States. From the Siberian railroad other railroads are now projected; mineral wealth is being uncovered; and English and French capital and American engineers will in the future work wonders with the country.

What Russia has long sought is an outlet to the ocean. This war is likely to give her benefits which she could never have asked and could only have fought for. Germany, defeated, will lose the control or monopoly of the Kiel Canal, and possibly the country around it which she took from Denmark. The Kiel Canal under international control will extend the Baltic Sea of the Russians and the Scandinavians most directly to the North Sea and the English Channel.

To the south Russia will have something to say in Asia Minor and much to say concerning Constantinople. Certainly her influence in the Balkan States and on the Bosphorus will be as great as she could desire. As long as the Turks remained loyal to England, Great Britain was bound to maintain their integrity and hold upon Constantinople and the Bosphorus. With the passing of the Turk Constantinople is in the hands of the Allies when they are victorious. Its final disposition is not yet clear, but the English people can see compensation in Egypt, Asia Minor, and Persia for any necessary Russian control of Byzantium.

While seeking one direct outlet by waterway, Russia may get two with the suicide of Germany and the destruction of her latest ally, the Mohammedan Turk.

Russia is beginning to be better understood throughout the British Empire and the world. The fear of an invasion of Western Europe by the Slav races is a bugaboo set afloat by Germany, who also propagates the bugaboo of a Japanese invasion of North America.

Russia is not a competing nation. She needs the capital and the brains of the outside world for her development, and in time she will offer the greatest field for world cooeeperation.

Japan wants to cooeeperate with Russia, and, indeed, with all European civilization. After the fall of Kiao-Chau she sent arms to Russia, and she stands ready to throw legions into the European field in defense of her English ally. Influential people in England are strongly urging the military authorities to permit the little Japs to join in.

Russia will keep faith with the Poles and the Jews and set up an autonomous Poland. But there is a strong resentment in Russia to-day because the Polish Jews misled the Russian army in the marshy grounds of East Prussia in the early campaigns of the war.

Russian military plans had to be changed and the field of war set farther south. Here Russia hopes to drive the five million people of Silesia back toward Berlin. This will awaken the Junkers of East Prussia and bring home to the people of Germany what the Prussian military machine really invites when it attempts a world-conquest.

Russia lacks military railroads and scientific means of communication. But just as America was surprised ten years ago to find the Japs, as the ally of England, giving, as the English predicted, "a good account of themselves," so the Russians as the allies of Great Britain may be found giving a very good account of themselves in this war. Russia is certainly unconquerable from either the Austrian or the German standpoint, and the smashing of Austria between Russia, Roumania, Servia, and Italy may be the real military campaign of this most Audacious War.

American engineers and diplomats familiar with Russia declare that, properly led, the Russian soldier is the greatest fighter in the world; and he is getting that leadership now.

The Russians expect the war will be over before next autumn, but Kitchener does not plan to end it then. He means to do this job thoroughly, and his plans are most comprehensive.

CHAPTER X

THE ENGLISH POSITION

A Quiet London—The Call to Arms—No Mourning—The Zeppelin Scare—German Spies—The German Landing—Kultur War Indemnities.

It is worth a winter trip across the Atlantic to stand with a London audience and hear it respond to the call, "Are we downhearted?" with a thunderous "NO!"

It is then you first realize that the British Empire is at war; and what that war means; and that that Empire has piped to its defense a free people inhabiting one fifth of the territory of the globe.

The British Empire has war upon its hands a major part of the time. It may be in the Soudan; it may be in South Africa. From some quarter of the globe war is almost always before the Empire. But a war summoning the whole British Empire to arms on land and sea,—that has not been dreamed of for a hundred years.

You expect to find in London an armed camp, the flags flying, the drums beating, the troops marching; an excited people discussing causes and effects of the military and naval programmes; military encampments with white tents over the plains. But you find nothing of the sort. If you attempt to motor in the country and figure on reaching a certain place in two hours, you may find it takes you four, as you are very likely to run into troops, companies, regiments, and armies in training, but mostly without arms and only partially uniformed. They are trudging the highways and the lanes of England from 5.30 A.M. until dusk,—rain or shine. Here is Kitchener's army being put into condition, with no fuss, feathers, or trumpet beats. The army is "rolling up" and "hardening up." But not on the tented campus. It is quartered in the towns and villages all over England, and board and lodging is regularly paid by the government.

There are no noticeable drum beats over England; no displays of bunting. Monuments, public buildings, and conspicuous corners, and, most conspicuous of all, the glass fronts of the taxi-cabs, bear signs calling the men of England to arms:—

"Fall in—Join the Army at once."

"Your King and Country need you. England expects that every man this day will do his duty."

"Enlist for the duration of the War."

"Enlist for three years."

"You are needed to fight for Honor and the Country's defense."

"No price can be too high when Honor and Freedom are at stake."

"Who dies if England lives?"

"He gives twice who gives quickly—join at once."

"'More men and still more until the enemy is crushed.'—Lord Kitchener."

Clarence W. Barron

And many more of the same tenor. Beyond these you will see little evidence in the London streets of an empire at war. Hotels are largely empty; managers very polite; restaurants must close at 10. P.M.; no after-theater supper at the hotels unless you are a guest. Men in khaki uniforms are more conspicuous; and bandaged heads, slung arms, and legs assisted by crutches are more noticeable than formerly.

The searchlights flash above the city; the street lights are shaded overhead in foolish fancy as a protection from aeroplanes or dirigibles. Curtains are closely drawn by police orders, in the houses and railway trains.

Yet one of the airmen who had been over London at night told me that the city was just as conspicuous as though it were wide open in illumination. Indeed, there is a general call among the Londoners for the police to let up and permit electric signs, lighted windows, and more light in the streets. But the only answer that came early in December was orders to turn down the lights further!

In Paris they turned on the lights, illuminated the streets, closed up the museums and galleries, buried their art and sent the Venus de Milo on a walk to some storage vault along with the banks' reserve gold. London's museums and picture galleries are wide open, and the endeavor to protect the streets from Germans peering down from above looks childish. The great strategy of the Germans consists of talking across the Channel about their plans for raiding England. I suspect that the English military authorities do not object. It encourages enlistment. When enlistment gets dull, the Germans stimulate it with some shells thrown on the English coast.

There are only two or three new plays in London this season; the great war-plays and dramas, and indeed the literature of this war, have yet to be written. Nearly all the new presentations for which London is so famous were set back on the shelf when the business of war started.

Most of the theater programs are revivals of old favorites, and a few of the theaters are still closed. All that are open begin promptly at 8 P.M. Five hundred English actors have gone to the front.

You have to make the circuit to find the heart of England at war, but you find it—horse, foot, and dragoons; men, women, and children. "Are we downhearted?" answered by a thunderous "No!" Then again silence, and turning down of the lights, and the steady work! work! work!

"Have you a bed here?" said Kitchener when he entered the War Office. "Never heard of such a thing here," was the response.

"Get one," said Kitchener; "I have no time for clubs and hotels."

Not only Kitchener but the whole staff camped down in the office, working days, nights, and Sundays, until Lady—turned over her house nearby to Kitchener and his staff.

"Where is—?" I asked of his next-door neighbor. The response was, "Oh, he is at the War Office, and gets a Sunday home with his family about once in six weeks." That family was not fifteen miles from London.

When a citizen has been suddenly notified that where he could formerly get a train for home every fifteen minutes, the railroad has been taken for military service, and he must get his supper in town, there is not the slightest word of complaint. He only wishes he could contribute more to the Empire.

I spoke with Lord K., of B—& Co., concerning the loss of his eldest son, as I had known Lord K. for many years. The manner, the gesture, the speech, in response, were all one, and brief; just an indication of sacrifice that had to be made for the Empire; and that sacrifice had only just begun; deaths in the family just honorable incidents in the life of the Empire.

Clarence W. Barron

You see crutches and broken heads in London, but you will see no mourning.

"Yes," said Lord C. to me, "the average income tax in England is now doubled until it is one eighth, or about 12 1/2 per cent, but my friends in the banking world have to pay an increasing supertax. I know many who must now give one quarter of their income to the government. They not only do it gladly, but expect it will be a half next year, and they will contribute that just as gladly."

From the top to the bottom in the Empire, all that is asked at the present time is a protected food and clothing supply, and everything else can go into "the cauldron of war."

"Did you ever see anything like it?" said an American banker in London to me. "Aren't these people wonderful? Did you ever see such resolution, such steady work, such sacrifices, such unity of empire?"

It was indeed worth a winter's trip across the ocean to see it.

Although the newspapers complained of the censorship, there was only one general complaint from the people in the British press. They wanted to know what the regulations were, or were to be, concerning self-defense when the Germans arrive in the country. Should a citizen without uniform take up arms against the invaders? Had he a right individually to shoot a German invader? Was the old rule that an Englishman's home is his castle, and that he has the right to defend it, now superseded by any rules of international warfare?

Some independent people of note were declaiming in the public prints that any German invader of England was a thief and a robber and that any weapons might be used to attack the invaders; and that there was no rule of warfare that could prevent an Englishman defending his home by any weapons against any foreign invaders.

Nevertheless the spirit of the people was, even under invasion, to respect law and order and rules of warfare, and be guided by the government as to all forms of individual or collective defenses. They simply wanted the rules promulgated.

The English are reconciled to Zeppelin raids from Germany, and rather expect them. But there is yet no unanimity in preparation or action. The Rothschilds have put four feet of sand on the roof of their building, but the amount of their gold in store must be incomparably less than that in the Bank of England, where no precautions are visible.

Trenches by the beaches and barricades by the highways are noticeable along the entire south and east coasts of England, but they are without stores or equipment. You run across these trenches in the moonlight as you journey about the country and for the moment you wonder for what purpose somebody dug those long ditches by the shore, and what the trench or irrigation scheme is. Your answer comes when you run straight into a timber barricade across the highway nearby. Then you look down the coast and see flashing searchlights, note the lights of steamers passing up and down the coast, and reflect that there is no universal law in war. The Channel steamers are carrying lights in the war area, but the North Atlantic steamers still cross the ocean without showing even port or starboard lights. The street cars moving in the English coast cities must, of course, be lighted and the streets must have some illuminant; but the railroad carriages, hotels, and private houses must draw their curtains. Yet railroad terminals and piers must have their lights, and harbors must have their searchlights. General service lights must be ablaze, but individual glimmers must be curtained. It reminds one of Cowper, the English poet, who, in the same kennel, cut a big hole for his big dog and a little hole for the pup.

The most talked-of war subject in England is the German spy system. It is estimated there were between 30,000 and 40,000 German spies, and many times this number of German reservists, in England at the outbreak of the war. For years

England has laughed over German theoretical discussions of how best to invade England, and German studies of English coast lines and country resources.

I heard years ago of a young Englishman who disputed in Berlin the war-office plans of his father's estate. He declared that he thought he ought to know the land where he was born and brought up as a boy, and that there were only two springs of water thereon, instead of three. The German general staff said their maps of England were correct and were not based on English authority. The young man found on his return to England that the German maps were correct and that his father's estate had three springs whence men and horses could be watered, although his family had never noted the existence of a third.

Two years ago some friends of mine were playing tennis in an English village and inquired the occupation of two young Germans, who seemed to be good tennis-players, but without family relations or settled business.

The response of the hostess was: "Oh, they are just two German spies of good education and charming manner looking over the country here, and we find them very useful in making up our tennis tournaments." It was looked upon as just a part of the German map-making plans, and England was an open book for anybody to map. Baedeker published the guide-books of the world: why shouldn't the Germans make all the maps of the world,—especially if German map-making were cheaper than English map-making?

A banker friend of mine found two young Germans in his village, with no other occupation than motoring the country over and making notes and sketches of cross-roads, railroad junction-points, important buildings, bridges, etc. He thought the authorities ought to know what was going on, but received a polite invitation from the local police to mind his own business. When once he lost his way on a motor-car trip, and ran across these fellows, he was very glad to get the right directions for the shortest way home. They knew more about the roads of that country than did the people who were born there.

About 20,000 German spies and reservists are in detention camps on the west coast, and on the islands. Even the German prisoners are kept away from the east coast, where it is expected the Germans may eventually struggle for their landing.

I have not the slightest confidence in any invasion of England by Germany, but I do not understand why German Zeppelins do not move in the darkness over the British Isles and drop a few bombs about the country at important places. It may be that the German Emperor is right in his calculation that such action would do very little damage, and would strengthen tremendously the enlistments and war-expansion plans of the English.

When West Hartlepool, Whitby, and Scarborough were bombarded by the German warships on the morning of December 16, the English excitement concerning it was only a small part of what an American would have expected. Not far from this bombarded coast is a summer resort town, where for many years a legend has existed that when in some future age England decayed and Germany came in, this would be the first landing-point.

An Englishman two or three years ago took it upon himself to find out how far this legend might have its base in any near invasion. He looked up the record and found that all the leading summer hotels and strategic points were in the hands of Germans. Then one day he quickly addressed his German waiter in his native tongue, demanding to know where his post was in that town in the event of hostilities. Promptly the German replied, "Down at the schoolhouse!" Further investigation showed that every reservist had his allotted place before and after the landing, and his place in the civic organization to follow. The Germans had also compiled lists of the people of property in that vicinity and exactly the character and amount of resources that could be commandeered from them.

If the Germans were free to map England, why should they not be free to map all its resources, individually as well as collectively?

I know a building in the heart of the London financial district that carries on its roof a Zeppelin-destroyer gun. A few days before I was last in this building a fine-looking fellow in khaki uniform entered in haste and asked the janitor to show him to the roof that he might quickly inspect that gun and see that everything was in order, as raids might be expected at any moment. Of course, he was taken to the roof, and his inspection quickly completed. Ten minutes later the London police were there to inquire for a man in khaki uniform.

The English officer said, "Very singular, we are ten minutes behind that fellow everywhere. He is the cleverest of all the German spies, and we are not able to catch him!"

If that spy had been caught in his English uniform inspecting English defenses, would not everything have been kept quiet in the endeavor to pick up the lines of his foreign communications?

In writing home from England, even to my family, toward the close of 1914, I thought it just as well to be brief and not too definite with any information. I had seen some of the censorship regulations and envelopes resealed with a paper bearing heavy black letters, "Opened by censor," with the number of the censor, showing that there are more than one hundred people engaged in this work; and also directions from the censorship that "responses to this inquiry must be submitted," etc., etc.

Nobody could believe until this war broke out and there descended upon peaceful Belgium not only armies and demands for their shelter, maintenance and food, and drink, but also huge demands for financial indemnification—war tax levies upon cities, towns, and provinces, with individuals held as hostages for their payment—that German war plans meant the looting, not only of nations and states, but of individual fortunes and properties.

It now seems that the march to Paris through Belgium and the imposition of a huge redemption tax upon Paris and France were but the preliminaries to larger demands upon London and England.

Indeed, judged by the demands upon Belgium, the German plans contemplated the transfer of the wealth of France and the British Empire to Germany; and such enslavement of these peoples as would make Germany rich, powerful and triumphant for many generations, if not forever, over the whole habitable globe. The German minister at Washington sounded a true German note when he asked who should question the right of Germany to take Canada and the British possessions in North America. Were they not at war, and if Germany were able, should she not possess them?

It had been understood before this war that countries were invaded under ideas of national defense. But possession of countries for the absorption of their wealth and the enslavement of their people, to work thereafter for the victors, was believed a barbarism from which this world had long ago emerged in the struggle for the freedom of the individual.

Clarence W. Barron

CHAPTER XI

ENGLISH WAR FORCES

The Men at the Front—The Recruiting—English Losses—Horses and Ships—War Supplies—Barring the Germans.

I really admire the English censorship and the manner in which it can withhold information from the English people, and I see the usefulness of much of the withholdings. You are some days in England before you realize that there are now no weather reports—not even for Channel crossings. Nobody really cared for them in London. Everybody there knew what the weather was, and nobody could tell what it was to be. If reports were printed, they would fool only the German Zeppelins; but cable reports might be quite another thing. So you can't cable your family: "Weather fine, come over."

Of course Germany should not be allowed to know the English forces, their exact number and distribution. I was told over and over again in good newspaper quarters in London that the English had only 100,000 men at the front, and did not propose to have any more until Kitchener led his army of a million men or more to the Continent next spring.

I, of course, said nothing, but I knew a great deal better, both from War-Office sources and from contact with the English officers in France.

It would not be right, although information was not given me in confidence, to attempt to name the exact number and position of troops Kitchener had on the Continent toward the close of December. But I may tell what anybody was free to pick up on French soil. I asked an English officer of good rank how many men the English had at the front and he responded promptly 220,000 at the front, and 50,000 on the lines of communication. He was right for that date in early December, but later more troops were sent over. Indeed, they were quietly going and coming all the time across the Channel, and, notwithstanding losses, the number at the front was being steadily augmented. There were also troops in training on French soil, and 550,000 in condition for shipment from England.

Kitchener is one of the greatest reserve-supply men in the world. He is a natural-born banker; he keeps his eye on his reserves fully as much as on his activities, and perhaps more so.

When he called for 100,000 troops the British public became weary and demanded to know how long before he would get them. This gave an impression throughout the world that English recruiting was very slow; but when forced to show down his hand, Kitchener had to admit that under the call for 100,000 men he had accepted many more and was still accepting.

Then they raised the call to a million, and in December Kitchener had more than 1,000,000 men under that call, but I was particular to ascertain that he had not made a call for a second million. It was all under the call for 1,000,000 men to arm.

But I did learn from authoritative sources that a house-to-house canvass, and millions of circulars sent out, had received responses that showed the War Office where the number of recruits, or men in training, could be quickly put above 2,000,000 the moment there was need or room for them.

When England sent her first expeditionary force of 100,000 men to the Continent there was no public report of how steadily it was augmented. The official announcement was simply that the line should not be diminished and that all losses should be made good.

An American acquaintance of mine, whom I found in France fighting in the uniform of the English, had made the declaration from his quick perception of the situation at the outset that if before January 1 the English should have sent over only another 100,000 men, they would have only 100,000 left there at the end of the year.

I found his estimate of losses correct. The English casualties at the end of 1914 were over 100,000,—killed, wounded, prisoners, and missing,—or fully the number of the first Expeditionary Force.

Yet every week and every month the forces of the English grew larger and never smaller. The filling in of the gaps and the augmentation of the English forces and their maintenance, munitions, and supplies was but the smaller part of the work of the War Office.

The great problem was to compass the situation as a worldwide war and summon and put into an effective fighting machine the resources of the Empire.

"Not alone the men but the machinery," said Kitchener, "must win this war."

England had to put into operation machinery, financial and diplomatic, machinery of men, guns, and transportation, belting the whole world and bringing the whole forward as a complete organization, yielding here and pressing forward there, but always firmly pressing to the one desired end—the crushing, crumpling and destroying of the war machinery of Germany. At the beginning England could not turn out 10,000 rifles a week; and a rifle can shoot well for only about

1000 rounds. Yet in December a single contractor in England was turning out 40,000 a week, and every possible contractor there and elsewhere had his hands full.

Kitchener must compass every detail from the rifle to the supply base; from the seasoned wood for that rifle right down to the number of troops he must have on the Continent when it comes to a settlement; for, says Kitchener, "You cannot draw unless you hold cards."

The broad sweep of the English preparations may be indicated by this: that when war broke out England not only commandeered horses in every city, village, and highway of England, taking them from carriages and from under the saddle, but started buying them over the seas. Of English shipping she gathered into her war-fold such a number of boats as I do not dare to repeat. She gathered in under the admiralty flag so many steamships from the mercantile marine that those which were found most expensive to operate were soon turned back into the channels of trade. With the many hundred steamers that she commandeered she set about transporting everything needed, including horses, from over the ocean.

The French bought their horses by the thousand in Texas and contracted at good prices for their shipment to Bordeaux. Steamship rates became almost prohibitive, and the horses arrived from their long journey in poor condition. England inspected the horses in America, paid for them, and then put them in charge of her own men on her own ships, and landed them by the shortest routes in England and on the Continent, in prime condition.

Although Germany had been buying liberally of horses in Ireland as early as March, when the long arm of Great Britain reached out there was no failure in her mounts for the cannon and cavalry divisions. For good horses at home and abroad she did not hesitate to pay as high as $350.

Americans should not forget that this war has brought about the greatest contraction in ocean tonnage that has ever been seen. I estimate that about one fourth of the world's oversea tonnage has been commandeered, interned, or put out of service. Before the war the Germans had nearly one eighth of the world's mercantile tonnage. That is now interned, destroyed, or tied up, outside the trade on the Baltic. As much more has been taken by the Allies from the mercantile to the war marine. It must also be figured that the Baltic and other seas hold locked-in ships, and the bottom of the sea likewise holds some more.

Considering the sudden demand upon the world's mercantile tonnage and its sudden curtailment, it is surprising that ocean commerce has not been more interfered with or made to pay even higher rates than the abnormal ones now existing.

Of war-tonnage, besides three superdreadnoughts purchased and four finished before the end of 1914, the British have under construction to be finished in 1915 ten battleships of from 25,500 to 27,500 tons, armed with 15-inch guns. The French have finished four of 23,000 tons, with 13 1/2-inch guns, and are finishing three more. The Russians are at work upon six of 23,000 tons, with 12-inch guns. The Japanese are building one superdreadnought of 30,000 tons, with 14-inch guns, and three battle-cruisers of 27,500 tons and 27-knot speed, with 14-inch guns.

Churchill, it will be remembered, figured that England could lose one battleship each month and still maintain her full strength. While the building of war-tonnage seems to be well in hand, there is no corresponding replacement of mercantile tonnage.

I have the highest authority for the statement that the world possesses no machinery at the present time to manufacture war-material at the rate at which the nations of Europe have been using it during the first hundred days of the war.

At one time the German armies were exploding 120,000 shells a day in France and Belgium. The response from the French alone was 80,000 shells a day, and General Joffre made a request that his supply be put up to 100,000 per day. This is for shells of all sizes, and the estimate to me was of an average cost of two pounds, or ten dollars, per shell. Some of the big German shells cost as high as $500 each. In some kinds of shrapnel, holding 300 bullets, there are more than thirty pieces of mechanism.

Within forty-eight hours after England declared war she had engaged the total output of an American manufacturer, whose machinery was an important part of the shell-making business. An American factory in Connecticut received orders for $25,000,000 worth of cartridges which would mean, at five cents a cartridge, 500,000,000 rounds of ammunition. I know of a single order to America from England for 10,000,000 horseshoes.

Through a single agency in America more than $150,000,000 worth of war-supplies was placed several weeks ago. I do not know whether this included a single order, of which I have knowledge, for 3,000,000 American rifles, delivered over three years at $30 a rifle, or $90,000,000. The company receiving this order had to work so quickly to install new machinery that old buildings were dynamited to clear the land.

Such orders to America are bound to tell upon our exports, and, combined with the advance in food-stuffs, the loss in cotton values by the outbreak of the war is offset more than twice over.

America must feel the effect of these orders when the goods go forward in increasing quantities. They are paid for as promptly as shipped. Many an American factory has been put on three eight-hour shifts for the day's work on these orders.

A Southern manufacturer received an order for 5000 dozen pairs of socks to be shipped weekly for six months. The price was under $1.00 per dozen, with ten per cent of wool in them. He complained that he was making only twenty cents per dozen profit, while if he had not been so anxious for the order, he might just as well have got a price that would have shown more than twice this profit.

In boots and shoes, England, instead of giving orders to this country, has been buying leather in America, and filling all her own factories. It is the policy of England to fill every workshop in her tight little island before she permits business to overflow.

To-day there are no unemployed in Great Britain, except in the cotton districts dependent upon German trade. Wage advances and overtime are the rule rather than the exception. The one country that the warring world must turn to for supplies is the United States, and that in increasing measure. Orders for $300,000,000 of war goods already received must be duplicated several times.

Every American automobile manufacturer able to deliver motor-trucks in lots of one hundred, has received his orders for shipments to the Allies.

Germany has now no base from which to get many important supplies. In a long contest the Allies will supply motor-cars, shells, guns, and ammunition to a far greater extent than Germany can manufacture them. Factories for this work are expanding in both Russia and America. The English do not speak against the Germans as a people. They believe them seriously misled by Prussian militarism, which they declare must be crushed absolutely.

Where formerly England was an open door to Germans and suspicions against German spies were laughed at, the bars are now sharply up. Most of the golfing clubs have voted to suspend the activities of members with German antecedents.

At the clubs in Pall Mall, notices have been posted requesting members not to introduce during the war Germans or those of German descent.

Membership on the Stock Exchange is not continuous as in this country, and at the March elections in 1915 there will be a dropping out of German names.

Clarence W. Barron

CHAPTER XII

ENGLISH WAR FINANCE

Protecting Trade and the Trader—How German Banks Paid—The English Loan—England's Wealth—The Income Tax—More Taxes.

A giant Atlas bearing the civilized world on its financial shoulders has arisen between the North and the Irish seas. That is the picture that stands at the opening of 1915, where before Germany had endeavored to stamp the label "Perfidious and degraded nation of shopkeepers."

Only the pencil of a Dore could sketch this giant and put him in figures of proper relief as, aroused from his pastime of trade and the acquisition of shillings, he summons with one hand the resources of the empire and with the other passes them out to needy warring nations, taking care all the while that the necessary dealing of exchange and commerce have the least possible disturbance.

Kitchener says the war may last for two years, but he is making preparations for three years, and must do this job so thoroughly that no repetition will be required.

If it is war for three years, then this mighty financial Atlas of England is preparing to write its name on promises to pay more gold than all the money-gold on the surface of the earth today. And England won't hesitate to do it if necessary—not for one moment.

How can she advance money to Russia, Belgium, France, and other countries at war or just going into the war, and ask no foreign assistance, no overseas help,—except to be let alone,—expand her home trade and wages, pay with a lavish hand, and still pile up real gold both at home and over the ocean?

The first answer is because she does expand trade; because she does pay and pay promptly; and because she does protect her own trade.

The United States does not protect its trade or its citizens anywhere in the world to-day. It shivers in war-time, and borrows of everybody else when it has a panic of its own.

There is only one way to make trade, and that is to pay and protect. England, through centuries of fighting to protect both trade and the trader, has learned the way to the highest freedom in both trade and finance.

Therefore, before this most Audacious War was set afoot England had a very small stock of coin gold but a very large stock of gold credit-bills.

For years England has held in her cash box from $1,800,000,000 to $2,500,000,000 of the commercial credits of the world. With goods and trade-honor behind these promises to pay gold, she had no need of the metal but only of command of the seas, that her gold might come in when needed. When the war broke out, $600,000,000 of these gold promises to pay were of German and Austrian origin. The big London bankers who had their names on the back of such acceptances could not in honor underwrite any more commercial bills. They knew their capital was involved in collection of those already out.

But Britain said the commerce of England must go on as well

Clarence W. Barron

as the war. The people who held these acceptances were promptly invited to turn them into the Bank of England, which held the guaranty of Great Britain behind it, and receive the money therefor; the discount rate after maturity to have 2 per cent added thereto, 1 per cent to go to the Bank for expenses and 1 per cent to the government for reserve fund to cover any losses. Of such bills $600,000,000 were promptly discounted.

I hear that two banks, the London City & Midland with its $525,000,000 of deposits, and Lloyds' Bank, both refused to rediscount. They believed the investments in commercial paper they had made were perfectly good, and that they were as well able as the Bank to wait for payment until one year after the war if necessary.

But to date more than half of these rediscounted bills have been paid.

It may be of financial interest to narrate how payments could be accomplished when by the King's orders there could not be any "dealings with the enemy" and payment to either side was forbidden by both. Yet the Dresdner Bank and other big German and Austrian banks have to date met fully one half their London obligations.

They were enabled to do this because their London branches were independent institutions whose independence was recognized by the British government. The London branches were thus liquidated, collecting in and meeting their obligations at maturity, so far as possible.

Liquidation in acceptances is one of the keys to the success of the English loan. While England had the ability before the war to discount $2,500,000,000 of acceptances, and with the present expanded base of the Bank would, without war, have the ability to discount $3,000,000,000, or three times our national debt, there is now no large business offering. The discount credits can therefore be measurably turned to the war-loan account. One of the biggest acceptance houses in London told me that the post-moratorium bills, or the new acceptances made after the moratorium, could not amount to more than 80,000,000 pounds, or $400,000,000.

With the liquidation on account of pre-moratorium bills and the absence of new business I should estimate that the London money market was able to take care of the 350,000,000 pounds loan put forth in November by the government without much regard to the investing community.

With expanding trade and confidence, English investment interests can absorb the major part of this huge loan before next summer, when another loan of about equal size must be put forth, according to present calculations. This second loan will probably be for three or four hundred millions pounds sterling, bear 4 per cent, and issue at par. The November loan was issued at 95 per cent and it was announced in Parliament that the Bank of England would loan the issue price at one per cent under the Bank rate.

That the loan was fully subscribed is not contradicted by the small fraction of discount soon quoted on the full-paid loan. One could fully pay the loan, taking the discounts on undue maturities and sell at a fraction under 95 and still make a profit.

I believe the estimate of an annual English surplus for investment of $2,000,000,000 per annum is far too low. This figure is upon the basis that only about 20 per cent of the river of interest, dividends, and profits flowing annually to British pocket-books is available for reinvestment.

In the present war stress and with economy practised to-day more by the capitalist classes than the laboring classes, the amount of money for reinvestment should be far greater than this.

English finance will cut its cloth according to the pattern. If there is only $2,000,000,000 per annum of surplus earnings to put into the war, that money will be spent; and if England has 50 or 100 per cent more, that money likewise will be spent, but spent so judiciously that the largest possible sum from it is kept in channels of English trade. The British Empire will work and finance the fight thus within a circle, and right on its own base.

The surprising thing is that it can be called upon to extend financial help to its allies. But everybody except Germany was caught absolutely unprepared. The war was early on French soil, tying up the resources of some of the richest provinces of France. Russia had so little thought of war that, as I have previously explained, she had deposited from her great gold reserve so that it had been loaned out on time and therefore was not available for the start of the war. Hence we have the spectacle of Russia gathering up 8,000,000 pounds sterling in gold and sending it to the Bank of England and, on this basis, borrowing of the Bank 20,000,000 pounds sterling.

Of course, this is good banking and good business and a good alliance. The Allies are bunching their war orders and credits, and England is entitled to hold the bag since she is carrying the financial burden.

England's war finance is not wholly measured in her expenses or loans to other countries. In a single issue of a London paper you can count daily reports of more than a dozen charitable funds connected with the war-work. These funds range all the way from "Aid to the Mine-Sweepers," "Gloves for the Soldiers," and the "Servian Relief and Montenegrin Red Cross Funds" up to the "Prince of Wales's Fund."

This last was over $20,000,000 before Christmas. The suddenness of this war may be illustrated by this fact: A friend of mine, who is managing director of a big English concern, has assumed the responsibility for seven years past of keeping in England one year's supply of everything that his company was likely to require from the Continent. This was at a cost to his company of many thousands of dollars. With dogged determination he stuck to the same policy for 1914, although in January of that year it was clear to him that Germany could not afford to go to war. While he was happy over his judgment, he admitted in conversation with me in December, 1914, that in January, 1914, the outlook was less indicative of a general European war than it had been for many years.

Thirty per cent of the workmen of his factory had gone to the war and his company was providing 250,000 pounds sterling a year to maintain the wages of the workmen at war up to the same amount as they would receive if they had stayed at home. He said that in one of his offices, of 80 men eligible for the work, 78 had enlisted, and, what was wonderful, the women were glad to take up the heavy work abandoned by the men,—something they would have refused to do in all ordinary times. On the whole, the output of this concern and its efficiency were materially increased, not diminished, by the war.

It is figured that troops at the front mean an expenditure of one pound per man per day, and that English troops in training mean an expenditure of not less than ten shillings per man per day.

The war expenses of Great Britain must thus be above one million pounds per day and steadily increasing. Indeed, the best economic estimate I have of the cost of the war to England is 500,000,000 pounds the first year.

While the English declare that they are fighting for their children and their grandchildren, they are not willing to leave to them the full load of the war-cost, and gladly do they assume all possible burdens in the present time.

The income tax, which began in 1842 at two pence in the pound, has now been doubled from one shilling and three pence to two shillings and six pence in the pound. This is on the average, and takes nearly one eighth of a man's income. There are very great variations in this tax. The rate I have given is the rate on dividends. Upon wages and salaries the tax is somewhat less.

The income tax is also apportioned over a three years' average. The supertax raises the contribution of the wealthy to one fourth of their incomes, although on the average it is figured to take only an eighth.

It is expected that the income tax may be further increased, possibly doubled, next year. I was not surprised therefore to find American millionaires with houses in London returning to New York and making sure of their American citizenship.

Every penny in the pound in the tax rate produces 2,500,000 pounds sterling, or $12,500,000, nearly one half the national income tax of the United States for 1913. Indeed, the English income tax for the year ending March 31,1915, is estimated to produce 75,000,000 pounds sterling, or about twelve times the income tax of the United States and from less than half the number of people. In other words, the income tax of Great Britain per capita is this year twenty-five times that of the United States.

But still the United States is really in no need either of income tax or of war-machinery. It is too late for the United States to prepare for any contest with the one nation that goes to war over tariffs—Germany.

After this war and a settlement of the Mexican situation, warships will be for sale at fifty cents on the dollar. Germany will have no navy of consequence, and England will reduce her present navy by at least one half, since her expansion of late years has been forced entirely by Germany.

CHAPTER XIII

GERMAN RESOURCES

The Food-Supply—War Expenses—The Copper Supply—The Call for Gold—No Outside Resources—The Human Sacrifice.

Counting Montenegro and Servia as two nations, there are now seven countries at war against Germany, Austria, and Turkey, and two more, possibly three, may join in within a few weeks. If Greece enters the battle-line, it will be ten nations against three. When Roumania and Italy join the Allies, as is now being diplomatically arranged, Germany will be completely surrounded, with Switzerland, Holland, and Denmark in a measure locked in and powerless to give aid or assistance to the Germans. Indeed, these three smaller countries and Scandinavia are practically locked in now, with the North Sea placed in the war zone, and Italy as well as Denmark and Holland shutting out all contraband goods for reexport to Germany and Austria.

Thus we have the spectacle of two nations of more than 115,000,000 people actually surrounded and besieged. Jointly these two nations in occupation of their entire territory could feed themselves from their own soil. They cannot be starved out, as in a besieged city, for lack of bread, meat, or drink. But the siege at the present time is not against the people of Germany and Austria: it is against the war-machine of

Germany. This war-machine can be starved out when cut off from gold, copper, rubber, and oils. If these cannot be cut off, then her men must be cut down.

Germany has raised by war-loan $1,100,000,000. She has spent this and $500,000,000 more besides. The financial strain is shown in her paper and exchanges at discounts outside her own border. Within her own realm she is piling up a gold reserve in her great bank, to sustain her expanded paper issues and her strained credit; but how is she securing the gold?

Calling a mark a shilling, or 25 cents, let us speak for a moment of Germany's finances in marks. After the war of 1870 she planted 125,000,000 marks in gold from the French indemnity in her war-tower at Spandau. In June, 1913, the Reichstag voted to double this to 250,000,000 marks in gold, the addition to be known also as the Spandau tower reserve, but to be placed in the Reichsbank and not counted in the bank reserves. There was also to be coined 125,000,000 marks in silver.

The whole was simply a stirrup-cup to enable Germany quickly to bound into the war-saddle with purchase of horses, food, and the light or perishable munitions of war which must be had at the outset and at a time when war panic first seizes the currency and supplies of a community.

The basis of German finance was 1,200,000,000 marks in specie, mostly gold, in the vaults of the Reichsbank at Berlin— the central bank of issue and bankers' deposits—with its 485 branches.

Before the war this metal reserve had been brought up to 1,400,000,000 marks. At the outbreak of the war, of course, the Spandau tower reserve in specie must have gone into the bank, and every metal reserve that the government could lay its hands upon likewise went into the bank. Germany then boasted a gold reserve approaching 2,000,000,000 marks. In this month of February the bank gold reserve was put well above 2,000,000,000.

Bank-paper issues meanwhile expanded by the billion.

The great contest in Germany is to maintain this bank metal reserve, and it is the task of Sisyphus and of herculean proportions. Outside of the United States, Germany has probably little, if any, credit to-day. She must pay in gold for what she buys from without, and from without she must get copper and oil. Lubricating oils are troubling her now quite as much as diminishing supplies of gasolene.

To get copper for munitions of war she can produce within her own borders 90,000,000 pounds. Of late years she has been importing from America 300,000,000 pounds per annum, so that electrification has been going on for many years all over Germany, and copper wires in telegraph-postoffice work scintillate in the skyline of the German cities. These can come down and be replaced with iron or aluminum. Of course, the first wires to come down will be the power-transmission wires. They can readily be replaced with aluminum, of which Germany is the parent producer. A very fair telephone service can be maintained with iron wires. Those who are looking for the exhaustion of Germany on a copper basis are reckoning without knowledge of German resources.

For petrol she can substitute benzol and alcohol, with some inconvenience. Germany is likewise the home and center of industrial alcohol, which it manufactures from surplus products. But when it comes to gold, there is the rub. Germany fixes a price of 20 cents a pound for copper within her own borders, but the government will pay 30 cents a pound to anybody who will deliver it to her from the outside. Indeed, I have heard of one lot of copper in Sweden for which 40 cents a pound was bid if the parties could ship it out across the Baltic.

I have a friend who was bid $5 a gallon for gasolene if he would land it within Germany, but such bids are not necessarily convincing. They may be made to fool the enemy. There are also stories of great underground storage-tanks of petroleum, owned by the government and concealed in the Black Forest, that have never yet been touched. It is inconceivable that Germany should plunge into a great war without having resources of copper and petroleum. But for all that is bought from without she must pay gold. No financiers know better the value of gold as the underpinning in finance than do the Germans.

Germany was very lavish with her gold at the start, and the French believed that it was an assistance in her military strategy. At the battle of Charleroi 50,000 German cavalry screened an unsuspected infantry force of 300,000 men and the French had to retreat; but that Maubeuge surrendered 40,000 men, without more fighting, gives rise in the French mind to suspicions of German gold. The anathemas of the French against their commander at Maubeuge make it much safer for him to remain a prisoner in Germany. The French caught one German wearing a French uniform but having upon his person one million francs. Of course, they shot him as a spy, but they were more incensed by the bribes he carried than by his uniform.

Everybody in Germany is called upon to lend a hand in maintaining the supply of gold for the government. The patriotism of the people was first appealed to. Then laws were passed. People are "requested" to give up their jewelry, to make a patriotic sacrifice of it for the Fatherland. Cards are printed in the newspapers urging the people for the sake of the Fatherland to bring all their gold into the Reichsbank.

So fine is the search for gold that wedding rings are given from the fingers of the women, and iron rings are substituted as badges of patriotism.

While every other nation on earth since 1900 has been accumulating gold in bank reserve, England alone has stood aloof and accumulated credit instead of gold. English financiers laugh at gold except as it can be made useful. They prefer to hold interest-bearing promises to pay gold. To-day England holds the keys to the world's gold outside of Germany, and I have a suspicion that she is not averse to American cotton going into Germany if it takes out the gold in return.

Germany is young as a banking, trading, and industrial nation. England insists that both men and gold must be at work. In Germany the gold reserve must be maintained and, with foreign trade cut off, men must be idle. In England both the gold and the men are at work. Labor was never better employed in England than to-day. The English policy in this wartime is to fill every idle hand with productive industry; to work the machinery day and night; and to keep the gold in England so far as is necessary and to keep it circulating in England. The national loss begins when you lose either the golden days of labor, the gold of the sunshine that makes the harvest of the valleys or the gold of finance and commerce.

When the Germans fought the French in 1870, 60 per cent of her people lived on the land. Now, forty-four years later, she is fighting the whole world, but only 30 per cent of her people live by the fruit of the soil.

That is the simple answer as to why Germany, a country besieged, cannot win against the world.

Germany has no sea-expansive ability, no foreign credit, no international reserves to carry out an offensive warfare. Her only possibility of success lay in a sudden and decisive march over the rich territory of France, the possession of Paris, and a huge indemnity tax levy as in 1871. The rest might have been easy. Hence the supreme military necessity for a quick drive through Belgium, the only open road to Paris. The size of the crime in Belgium has shown the supreme financial necessity. There was no military necessity for the outrage against the free Belgian people—only the economic necessity.

There is nothing left for Germany but a defensive warfare, a warfare now conducted upon foreign soil just over her own borders—the burden upon the enemy, the supply base near at hand.

Germany must reduce and conserve her shell-fire. The Krupp works have no ability to turn out daily the number of shells that Germany was exploding, and the United States in its own arsenals could not in a year make a week's supply of shells at the rate at which they were being exploded from Switzerland to the English Channel.

Greater than progress in the arts of peace is progress in the art of war. We have read in the American papers of a most wonderful new French shell that in bursting paralyzes and destroys life so instantly that all the living things within so many yards are, in a flash, set rigid in position as though manufactured for Jarley's Wax Works, the officer standing in position with uplifted arm, yet dead, the soldier by the window with a cigar in his fingers, a smile on his face, stone dead.

I was informed that the effectiveness of this shell was not due to its poisonous gases but to the fact that, instead of being filled with bullets, it was charged with a wonderful new explosive.

For the development of the science of war twelve months in the line of battle is worth in new inventions ten years of peaceful military study. A three years' warfare for which the English are planning is likely to put Germany's thirty years of "peaceful" war preparation quite in the shade, so far as practical results are concerned.

I hear of new and more powerful mortars and cannon, wonderful new rifles, now being manufactured by the million from secret plans, and new guns to bring down Zeppelins, that it is not useful to discuss here.

In the first six months of this war, the German casualties must be well up toward 2,000,000. A million of the injured may go back to the firing line.

But in killed, seriously wounded, missing, and prisoners, Germany must be losing at the rate of 2,000,000 men a year, and the forces of destruction against her will increase rather than diminish. That she can lose at this rate for three years and have anything left worth consideration as a military power is beyond reason.

Nevertheless, when I spoke with a very prominent American, now in a responsible position abroad, he said: "The Germans have food and supplies, and they have an idea; and the only way to overcome that idea is by their destruction. The South had no resources for a three-year or four-year war, but it had an institution, an idea, and a determination. If you will recall it, at the close of the war there were practically no men left in the South. This war will be over when the fighting men of Germany have been killed off."

I have so much respect for the business, mathematical, and scientific mind of Germany, that I cannot believe she will prefer the destruction of the German people, individually or collectively, to the destruction of the German war-machine which set on this war.

I make the following estimate of the casualties—killed, wounded, missing, and prisoners—of the warring powers, omitting Turkey and Japan, up to February 1, 1915:—

German.......1,800,000
French.........1,200,000
Russian........1,600,000
Austrian 1,300,000
Belgian 200,000
Servian 150,000
Montenegrin....20,000
English........110,000
Total 6,280,000

Not in a hundred years, or since the Napoleonic wars of 1793 to 1815, has there been any war approaching these casualties now reaching in six months to six millions.

A remarkable statistical fact concerning the war, which I ran across in London, was a computation that the deaths in the navy were substantially equal to those in the army, from the beginning of the war up into November. Of casualties in the army, only about 10 per cent are deaths. There are few wounded to be returned home from a naval disaster. When the English army had suffered about 60,000 casualties, making about 6000 men killed, at the same time from the naval service 6000 boys in blue had gone down to watery graves.

CHAPTER XIV

IS IT THE PEOPLE'S WAR?

German Socialism—German Unity—A Reverse Political System—Business Men without Political Influence—A Voice from the People—The German War Lord.

In America there is no greater conflict of opinion than over the question of the relations of the German people to the present war. There are those who declare most emphatically that when the German people once understand this war there will be revolution in Germany, uprising of the socialists, and the sure overthrow of the Hohenzollern dynasty.

Such opinions are not well based, and their authors do not understand the German temperament, the principles of German government, German organization, or German Socialism.

Socialism in Germany is neither of the destructive order of that in Russia, nor of the wild varieties found in America; nor has it even the order of the Socialism of England. Twenty years ago the Socialism of Germany might be recorded as against the invasion of Belgium, and the bonds of Socialism existing between Belgium, France, and Germany might have interfered with the war programme.

But Socialism in Germany has passed the stage of laboragitation. Indeed, it has been transformed in the reign of the

Clarence W. Barron

present Kaiser from agitation against capitalism within the empire to agitation for the expansion of Germany in the territory of its neighbors throughout the world, that German labor may, through German arms, enter into and possess the land without. German Socialism is thus allied with German militarism, and it has also become the respectable party of opposition in the Reichstag. The middle classes of Germany of late years have voted for Socialistic candidates whenever they disagreed with the government. It is the party of protest and of opposition. It is a party of the empire, not of any world socialistic movement.

Germany is thoroughly knit together in support of its government and its Kaiser. The German people do not seek a constitutional government like England, or a republican form of government like France or the United States. They believe their situation and safety in the middle of Europe call for a more autocratic form of government, and one not too quickly responsive to popular sentiment.

Germany was made by Bismarck and the armies of Von Moltke supporting the Hohenzollern dynasty. This made Prussia the center of Germany industrially, financially, and as a military power, and at the heart and seat of power, in both industry and finance, sits the same dynasty. The Emperor is the center of industry, finance, and military power,—three degrees of empire, each distinct in itself, but each intertwined with the others, but so intertwined that the word of power, command and influence comes down from the military seat of power through finance and into industry. Industry does not speak back through the powers of finance to the military center. The flow of the German dispensation of power or of governmental organization runs downward from the Kaiser. No power goes up from the people or industry or finance to the war lord at the center.

The Germans know no other system of government. Outside of Prussia, in the more than thirty states of Germany, there was the local reign. Now over all is the reign of the Kaiser. The present generation has seen a united Germany become great among the nations of the earth. The English-speaking people cannot appreciate the feudalism and the fealty of the German people to their war lord. They say, "Are not the German people great thinkers; do they not know that the power of government is from the governed?" It is inconceivable to them that the Germans should have a reverse system.

My last word from Germany was with an American lady who has been more than one hundred days nursing the wounded from the battle-line, and she, singular as it may appear, assisted on both sides of that battle-line. She assisted to dress the wounds of French soldiers where the lacerations of shrapnel had broken one entire side of a human system, face, eye, ear, jaw, arm, leg; yet that soldier lived. She dressed wounds where more than twenty bullets pierced a single human frame. Yet that soldier will go back to the front. French boys in their 'teens had died in her arms at the hospital,—the hospital where thousands of wounded pass through every month,—and she had taken back to the parents in Paris the dying message. She had been in the German and the French trenches on the line of battle. She had crossed the lines and been under arrest. She had seen the horrible picture of freight-loads of German corpses on German railroads,—corpses unhelmeted, with uncovered faces, but in boots and uniform, tied like cordwood in bunches of three and standing upright on their way to the lime-kilns. She had nursed the wounded German soldier in his delirium, crying in German, which she well understood, over the horrors which still pursued him as he remembered the face of the wife and saw the agony of the children as he stood in line and by direction of his superior officer shot the husband dead. He moaned in his delirium over the picture. The faces of the wife and children haunted him, but he cried out that his superior officer had ordered him to do it; and she said, "No, these people are not responsible; the dogs of war have driven them as sheep into the slaughter-pens. They are beaten, but fight for the Fatherland. It is their duty and they obey."

And how has it all come about? Simply thus: The Saxon was a

Saxon, the Bavarian was a Bavarian; each suddenly found himself a German and part of a world-power. Bismarck and Von Moltke had a policy for the Hohenzollerns; it was a united Germany, and they left it a defensive Germany.

There was not in the brain of Bismarck or of Von Moltke, or of the Emperor under whom they prosecuted the wars against Austria, Denmark, and France, any idea of Germany as the Conqueror of the world.

"Never be at enmity with the Russian Bear," was the saying at the time of Bismarck and before. "Always contrive that yours shall be a defensive war; let the other party attack," was the declaration of Bismarck.

The policy of Bismarck was: "If you have an enemy, make friends with all the other powers, so that your enemy be isolated diplomatically and politically."

The present Kaiser has reversed every one of the great policies of Bismarck and of his ancestors that made a united and great Germany.

There is not a language in the world to-day outside the Teutonic that speaks the praise of Germany. Defensive German alliances are broken because the present Kaiser insisted that offensive and defensive are one and the same. In offensive action the Triple Alliance breaks; while the Triple Entente becomes, for defense, nine nations instead of three.

The German people are not responsible for this situation. Their form of government has not yet permitted full, free, and effective expression of opinion; nor does the German seek full political expression. He loves his fireside and his family, and prefers his home ease and philosophy. He has confidence in his Kaiser and his government; and his whole training for a generation has been to make him an obedient part of a military power.

It is gratifying to find that not the German people, but the German Kaiser, is responsible for this war; and it is also gratifying to find that there are doubts as to his full mental responsibility.

I have had closer associations with the German people than with the French, and have liked them better as a people: they are so industrious, efficient, and ambitious in the world's work. I know the German country better than the country of France or England. I think I understand something of the over-self-sufficiency of the English, and I have no prejudice against the Germans, or even their form of government, which may be better adapted to their needs than a broader democracy. But of the German modern war-philosophy the world outside can hold but one opinion. It might have been supported as a purely tentative or speculative philosophy, but it could have been promoted in practice only by a crazy ruler. I was not therefore surprised to find circulated in Paris an article by an American physician which I had permitted to be published in America at the outbreak of the war, showing the mental weaknesses and hereditary taints of Germany's war lord.

I recall him from memory of bygone years, and as I saw him in Berlin when his grandfather was still on the throne—a young man of about twenty, returning from the races and dashing through the Tiergarten holding the reins of six coal-black horses.

I said to myself: "That young man will cut a dash yet." And I still see, in higher light than before, those six coal-black horses—the horses of death.

Recently I read pages of his writings, speeches, and declarations, and there is not for the world an uplifting or new thought within them all. What appears to be new is the echo of an age that was supposed to be long past—when might was rule and valor was religion.

"There is but one will, and that is mine," said the Kaiser, addressing his soldiers; but it has been the keynote to his diplomacy wherever it has appeared, either in pushing a commercial treaty on Russia in her hour of distress, forcing Italy into the Triple Alliance, or dictating the terms of the Austrian ultimatum to Servia, so that it would be impossible of fulfilment.

What is there of world-progress in the declaration of the present German Emperor, celebrating the two hundredth anniversary of the Kingdom of Prussia,—

"In this world nothing must be settled without the intervention of Germany and of the German Emperor."

CHAPTER XV

THE GERMAN POSITION

An Aggressive Germany—The Logic of It—The War Party Supreme—A War for Business—What Confronts Germany—Her Finish.

A mighty nation surrounded and besieged, yet still fighting on foreign soil, is the position of Germany to-day. Her triumph would mean, not alone a European conquest, but a world-conquest. Her defeat within a reasonable time does not mean her destruction or dismemberment. It means only the destruction of Prussian militarism and that theory of national existence into which the German people have been led under the present emperor, that theory which teaches:—

"War and courage have done more great things than Charity."

"What is good? All that increases the feeling of power; the will to power."

"The weak and debauched must perish, and should be helped to perish."

This is the philosophy, the teaching and the language of Nietzsche and on it Treitschke and Bernhardi founded their war propaganda.

Clarence W. Barron

When Emperor William II ascended the throne and became the "All Highest War Lord," he found himself at the head of two great Germanys: a military Germany arising from the Prussian conquest of France in 1870, by which more than thirty states had been welded into a compact unity of military order, commercial tariffs, railroad transportation, and national finance; and an industrial Germany forging ahead in the commercialism of the earth at a pace exceeded by no other nation.

Bismarck and Von Moltke had made a Germany for defense. The railways did not flow to the ocean for the interchange of commerce. They ran primarily east and west to the Russian and French frontiers for military reasons; but never for attack, always for defense. It was expected that France would revive and again seek to try issues with Germany. In this she might possibly be assisted by Russia. Hence the German plans were for defense against these two countries.

As Germany developed in industry, the military caste receded relatively. Bankers, merchants, shippers, and traders came to the front. Railways bent the traffic of the country to the sea, and harbors and ports of commerce grew with rapid strides.

"What a wonderful business man is the German Emperor!" said the world. "He advertises Germany all over the earth by the spiked helmet and the rattle of his sword, but never war seeks he." The world must now revise this opinion.

German unity gave rise to German efficiency and German thoroughness, and to a demand for a larger German unity. The whole German-speaking race must be put together and bound together. Germany must expand over the seas, in colonial empire, and by tariffs of her own making. This meant that the Germans must have dominion on sea as well as land. Alliances must first be cemented with Austria and her neighboring states. Italy must be dragged into a triple alliance; and the small Balkan States must be tied up with Austria, that through an alliance with Turkey, Germany might reach not only the

Mediterranean but the waters of the Pacific. This must happen before the great try-out for the mastery of the seas.

Now, the central point in the study of Germany under the present Kaiser is the naval programme for over-seas conquest, which was originated entirely by the present Kaiser. It was he and no other who aimed to turn defensive Germany into aggressive Germany. He has been the author from the beginning of the entire naval programme.

Such a plan must take cunning and strategy covering years. It must proclaim peace to the world but rouse all the fighting blood of the German-speaking race. The spirit for world-conquest must be stimulated in all literature and art, in education, and commerce; with the individual and the family. The danger of Germany must be pointed out. The greatness and rightfulness of her ambitions in the world must be brought forward and educated into the blood of every growing German.

While to the outside world steadily proclaiming peace, the Kaiser was as steadily inculcating war and the principles of war into every avenue of German thought and philosophy.

The Germans are nothing if not logical and scientific. They must therefore find a reason in philosophy and in the facts of history for their national programme. Those who found these reasons and logically set them forth were hailed as the great philosophers and educators of Germany. The logic was simple. It was that all history and all progress had been made by war; that peace-loving races decayed, and finally perished, and their places were rightfully taken by the younger, braver, sturdier, and hardier fighting races.

"Let your superiority be an acceptance of hardship." "Die at the right time." "Be hard." "What is happiness? The feeling that power increases, that resistance is being overcome." Nietzsche thus talked the principles of this philosophy; a something entirely apart from the principles of the Christian religion, but an absolutely philosophical, modern paganism; a worship of power, the assertions of one's individual and national self—"The Will to Power."

Treitschke taught it to the youth of Germany as applied to war,—not the necessity for defense but the justice and the righteousness of aggressive warfare. The Emperor and his court hailed these teachings with great acclaim. Chamberlain, an Englishman, printed a book to show that all good things were German; that the great Italian art-workers were German; that Christ himself was of German origin.

The teachings of Christ were repudiated by Germany, but His greatness in world leadership must be claimed for Germany. Had not all the poets given Him the German countenance and complexion, even light hair and blue eyes? The German Emperor bought presentation copies of this book by the thousand.

If you think the picture is over-drawn, get a copy of Chamberlain's "Foundations of the Nineteenth-Century Civilization."

There are those who acclaim that all these teachings were never meant for war; that the Germans, outside of Prussia, being a phlegmatic, home-loving, non-military people, needed to have their patriotism stimulated with "war talk" and national ambitions.

Now there are those who see that it was all part of a cunning propaganda for a world-conquest; that Germany was cultivated industrially and financially to give base for military operations.

But most carefully have the business men of Germany been excluded from the war councils. I asked one of the best-informed men in the diplomatic cycles of Europe, whose business all his life has been to travel from country to country studying the languages, thought, and customs of all people, west of Asia and north of Africa: "Are the German bankers and business men to have no say in Berlin as to peace and war or the military policy of the empire?" His response was emphatic: "Not one word; they would no more be allowed expression of opinion in the inner councils of military Germany than would a rank foreigner from the farthest part of the earth. Still in Germany is the business of trade apart from the business of government."

The world may now see that the business of Germany was war from the beginning under Kaiser Wilhelm II, and that Germany was to be made great on land and sea by the sword of war hacking the way for German commerce, German tariffs, and German commercialism. The old feudal idea of trade expanded and supported by a war lord has been the idea of Germany since the pilot, Bismarck, was dropped by the young Emperor from the ship of state. War for aggression, war for business, war for German expansion, has been the scheme. That these plans were interrupted and the war precipitated sooner than expected was most fortunate for American civilization and all civilization, west of Germany.

It was the Kaiser who changed the terms of Austria's ultimatum to Servia, making them impossible of fulfillment, and then cunningly slipped away on a water-trip with the fastest German cruiser behind him, that he might come rushing back and cry, "Peace, peace!" while he fenced off every peace proposal from effectively reaching Austria. Servia was willing to agree to every demand of Austria except that which involved a change in her constitutional government, with which she could not comply in the allotted time; but even this she was willing to discuss. The Kaiser gave Russia twelve hours to demobilize, and then declared war on her five days before Russia even withdrew her minister from Vienna.

While the Germans have gone to war to possess the land and dominate the business of their neighbors, they have not gone to war as savage tribes, seeking blood and human sacrifice as an end in itself.

I have not dealt with German atrocities in Belgium or France. War is atrocious, and you cannot move millions of men to the slaughter of their fellow men without revealing a certain percentage of crimes kindred to murder.

In due time, all the atrocities of this war may be shown up in photographs which have been taken. The Carnegie Peace Foundation is circulating photographs showing the atrocities in the Bulgarian wars. It might be much more timely for them to circulate photographs showing the horrors and atrocities of human sacrifice in this most audacious war.

Previous chapters have shown how German diplomacy slipped, how the German secret service had gathered the facts of the military, financial, and political weaknesses of Russia, Great Britain, and France, yet with no ability to value properly the spirit of the peoples behind this military unpreparedness. Germany has been described as "System without Soul." It remains only to show the relative weaknesses of Germany, and why she cannot win this war.

The Allies can reach round the world for men, war-supplies, and financial assistance. Germany can get no more men, no more gold, no more outside war-supplies. She must manufacture and be self-sustaining.

In the first six months of the war Germany has raised a loan of 4,400,000,000 marks, or about 1,100,000,000 dollars, promptly and patriotically taken by her people.

But international bankers inform me that every dollar of this and fifty percent more was gone before January 1, 1915. This is also indicated by the expansion of her paper money and her efforts to maintain the gold basis under that paper.

As this is regarded as a life-and-death struggle for Germany, the jewelry in the Empire must go into the melting-pot.

I can well credit the reports of copper household utensils and building materials going into the melting-pot for the copper of war.

And of rubber, for which there is no substitute, I hear that above three dollars a pound is being bid in Germany, or about four times the price in the United States.

Still, the scarcity of gold, copper, gasolene, or rubber, or all combined, might not force Germany to sue for peace.

What I give a final verdict on is the tremendous human sacrifice that is exhausting both Austria and Germany. I do say from good sources that in the first twenty weeks of the war the German casualties—wounded, prisoners, missing, and killed— were above 1,700,000, while Austrian casualties are now approaching a million and a half.

In the first six months of the year Germany and Austria will have suffered not less than three million casualties. Of course, more than half these people are wounded, who may go back to the firing line. But the three hundred thousand and more dead will never go back; and many vitally wounded and many cripples will be hereafter useless in peace or war; and the prisoners that are exchanged with France through Geneva are under pledge and mutual government agreement not to take up arms again.

I have also more confidence in the Russian position, numbers, supplies, and strategy than is generally possessed in America.

We hear in the press reports of generals at the head of the armies in Russia and France. We do not hear of the wonderful younger generals that war is developing, and who are coming forward more rapidly there than from any similar developments under the bureaucracy of Germany.

The two greatest military strategists the war has developed are not in Germany or England. They are in Russia and France, and their names have not yet crossed the Atlantic in the press reports.

However long Germany may fight on, offensively or defensively, her retreat must begin this year. Then the world will be increasingly interested in the terms of peace.

Balfour, the English statesman, says privately, "I know the people look for the dismemberment of Germany, and some look for her destruction, but this is not the intelligent opinion or intelligent desire. Germany is an indispensable part of the world's industrial, commercial, financial, and political organization. To destroy Germany would be a world loss." The opinion of eminent political and financial people in England is that Germany can never repair the total damage she may inflict. So far as England is concerned, next after the destruction of Germany's war-power, giving insurance of a European peace, comes first the indemnification of every financial loss that Belgium suffers. This is now estimated at from $1,500,000,000 to $2,500,000,000.

What there will be left over in the way of Germany's ability to pay, aside from the Kiel Canal, Alsace and Lorraine, and German Poland, is problematical.

To have Germany able to pay even a part of the damage she is inflicting upon the world, she must be put back upon her industrial feet. Therefore, I have declared, when asked about this matter, that in the end England would be found the best friend of Germany. But conquered and destroyed must be the Prussian war-machine of aggression, or crumbles the art and industry of republican France and the democracy of English speech, thought, and government.

CHAPTER XVI

THE LESSONS FOR AMERICA

Wealth is National Defense—Gold Mobilization—Food Supplies International—No Financial Independence—Tariffs as War Causes—Are We in a Fool's Paradise?

The lessons for the United States and for all America from this war are so many that it is difficult to arrange them in order.

The first lesson is that nations can be no longer isolated units. A hundred years ago the United States desired to be free from Europe,—from its political system, its wage system, and its social system. To-day the United States cannot desire to be freed from any country in the world. Its Panama Canal, its demand for a mercantile marine, for countries to take its cotton and cotton goods, and its inquiry as to where it can get potash salts and chemical dyes, all show the interrelation of modern business which has broken all national boundaries.

England is talking to-day of a closer federation in her empire to follow this war. She is asking why she alone should be the protector of the seas, and of the peace of Europe, not only for herself and her colonies, but for the whole world. She is already talking of a federation for the empire by which Australia, Canada, etc., will have direct representation in Parliament, and assist directly in bearing the burden of the maintenance of peace. I doubt if a British federation will

Clarence W. Barron

strengthen the British Empire. Mutual interest is the great federator. The unwritten Constitution of England has more binding force than the written Constitution of the United States. The Triple Entente is stronger and more binding than the Triple Alliance.

The whole world is interested in the maintenance of peace, and it should not be the business of any one nation or empire to maintain the peace of the world.

Secondly, if the burden is put upon England to maintain the peace of the seas and the peace of Europe, she must have a growing empire to support that burden.

Already the English people see the spread of her influence which is to follow this war and make Cecil Rhodes's dream of a Cape to Cairo railroad a reality for Africa. Egypt, Palestine, and Asia Minor are hereafter to be restored in fertility and give a new civilization to the shores of the eastern Mediterranean.

Is it to be assumed that with the new development for Africa and Asia, Europe is going to abandon her interest on the continents of America?

Will not the very force of these developments make a foundation for European developments in North and South America?

Have we not seen that the British Empire has still some interest in the Panama canal? Is it to be supposed that when peace succeeds in Europe, and the European nations lie down together for another period of mutual development, France will make no inquiry concerning her $800,000,000 of property in Mexico? Or that England will adopt Mr. Bryan's idea that any Englishman or American who goes into Mexico cannot look for any protection from his home government?

I believe that Lord Cowdray is to-day the foremost business man in England. He represents oil lands in Mexico worth intrinsically more than $100,000,000. Is it the policy of the British government to say, "Cowdray, forget it, and come over and develop Mesopotamia; living is unsettled in Mexico, and Uncle Sam has told 'em to fight it out"?

A third lesson the United States will receive from this war is the value of large units in business and the value of national wealth as national defense.

Instead of trying to pull down wealth and individual accretions of wealth, the country will recognize that all savings and every increment of fortune, small or large, are for the ultimate benefit and for the prosperity and defense of the whole country.

In this war Russia is poor in railroads, and the advantage that Germany has held over her in Poland is more by reason of the German railways than the German armies. Railways are products of wealth and individual capital, and the sooner the United States learns this lesson, the better.

A fourth lesson for the United States from this war is the value of gold in bank reserves, and the value of ability to mobilize quickly such reserves. No nation in the world to-day is more closely tied to every other nation than by the invisible strings of gold. Every nation in the world has an interest in the gold supply and the gold reserve in bank throughout the world.

There are those in England who still believe that this war will be the supreme test of the gold monometallic base for money and banking. There is no thought as yet that Germany, if driven off the gold base, will seek a silver base. It has always been declared by the bimetallists that the successor of gold monometallism will be paper, and Germany is expected to go upon a paper rather than a silver basis.

In exchange operations German paper is about 8 per cent discount, but exporting gold or buying or selling gold at a premium is by law forbidden. All are penal offenses.

England can stand upon a gold basis because she commands the gold promises to pay, but in war time she can threaten the stability of the monetary systems of many countries. The United States saved its gold base by closing the Stock Exchange, but the South American countries were quickly in distress for gold.

To put India on a gold basis a few years ago, a tax was levied on Indian silver imports with the result that India has absorbed $400,000,000 in gold from England in the last five or six years, and where payments to India were formerly one-quarter gold and three-quarters silver, they are now one-quarter silver and three-quarters gold.

All these matters are being sharply watched by the English economists.

A fifth lesson we may draw from the war is the necessity for a larger official representation abroad. It was fortunate that before the outbreak of the war the American embassy in London had been moved to larger quarters by the gardens west of Buckingham Palace.

The strain that was thrown upon that embassy for information, passports, transportation, etc., was something terrific. United States statutes allow this embassy only three secretaries, but it had to use eight, and the work continued until 3 A.M., and sometimes 5 A.M. There was only one relief in the situation and that was in a study of the queer characters one finds abroad, insisting that they are representative Americans. Some of the people demanding free transportation back to America declared their residence to be in Hoboken, but could not tell if Hoboken were nearer New York City than to San Francisco. It was a great temptation for some people to get out of the war zone and into America at the expense of Uncle Sam. The amount of business transacted by this embassy may be illustrated by the fact that the cable tolls alone for several months cost more than the former total expenses of the embassy.

Still another lesson from the war that America must learn is that food supplies are now not national, but international. We have seen the price of sugar in the United States jumping up and down in a commercial battle between England and Germany almost before their clash at arms.

Before the war, 80 per cent of the sugar consumed in England was produced in Germany. England, under her free trade policy, had permitted German beet sugar interests, fattened upon a government bounty, to destroy the refinery interests in the south of England. The Island gained by the trade because her refineries were turned into sugar canneries. Jams and marmalades therefrom expanded her foreign trade. Germany, however, at the outbreak of this war, proposed to cut off, or tax heavily, England's sugar supply. Into the markets of the world went the British Treasury and in a few days the government was in command of an eighteen months' supply of sugar for the whole of Great Britain. Down went the price of sugar in Germany, and now the government is taking measures to restore prosperity to her sugar interests by a reduction in beet-sugar plantings. The English government is selling sugar in England at a loss, as a war measure, and will not permit sugar purchases in any country where Germany sells her sugar.

Nothing but the strain of war could have induced the Bank of England to count a hundred million dollars in gold sent from New York into Canada as a part of the Bank's metal reserve.

There is now no reason why this relation should not continue. Why should fifty or a hundred million in gold be sent across the ocean in the spring, to be returned in the fall? The world is going to be still more a unit in finance hereafter. It has taken a generation to educate the world to the right of the individual in the common fund of money, so far as money is needed to effect transfer of credits. This is the keynote in our Federal Reserve act: that business has just as much right to regulation promoting safe and smooth credits as it has to national regulation promoting safe and sound transportation.

Clarence W. Barron

Out of this war must arise better international relations, and they comprise not alone the relations of peace, but closer relations to international transportation, as respects both ships, international money, and international credit.

While many people are looking for financial independence between nations, the United States taking back from Europe in the next three years the larger part of the $6,000,000,000 of American securities owned abroad, it is quite possible that the opposite will take place: a greater interrelation, not only in credits but in investments.

If nations are to be more closely knit together hereafter, it will be not alone in alliances of peace, but in financial alliances in security ownership.

It is far better for both Europe and America that, instead of Europe selling its American securities, America should buy European securities—first, acceptances, making a basis for credits and international purchases in connection with the war; and later, American investment in the funds of foreign nations. It may be that before this war is over many European nations will have to appeal to America with their loans.

If France could see her way clear to put out a long-term loan at 5 per cent instead of short-term loans at this rate, there should be a good investment field for it in America.

Russia is an unconquerable country, and her securities at a good rate should be attractive for some American capital.

There is no reason why the 3 per cent bonds of Germany should not soon be investigated for investment purposes in America. The German debt is very small and, however long the war may continue, German bonds will ultimately be paid. They are quoted now at about 70, and, with the discount on exchange, they may be purchased from America at nearly 60, or to get 5 per cent on the investment, to say nothing of possible appreciation toward par in the future.

One may well believe the Germans to be misled in this war, and yet properly await opportunity to purchase at the right time their outstanding national bonds when these can be purchased so much more advantageously toward the end of the war than in the beginning of the era of peace, which must in time follow. Is it not just as neutral to purchase German bonds from the Germans as to purchase ships or our own railroad shares from Germany?

A great and primary lesson for the United States is in a thorough understanding that this war was caused by tariffs. The United States is the home of protective tariffs. The sentiment under a protective tariff is national selfishness. England has bought in other markets wherever she could buy cheapest, and has kept her ports open to the cheapest markets. This may be her selfishness.

It may, however, remain for the United States, while maintaining a protective tariff, to look to larger international relations and admit reciprocal trade-relations. There is a wide field for study here in connection with this war, for the same spirit—the wresting of commercial advantages by tariffs without regard to the fellow nation—is in many countries.

We aim in this country to boycott foreign manufactures with the declaration that we should give all the advantages to labor in this country, and keep our money at home. But what do we think when we find that Germany has for years run a boycott against every American enterprise?

America's great International Harvester Company, which has made and promoted the great agricultural inventions of the world; the Singer Sewing-Machine Company, that spreads its manufactures over the earth, and brings back the returns to the United States; all American motor-car companies, all American tobacco interests, and, in fact, all foreign companies, are boycotted, or barred, or worked against, throughout Germany. Placards in shop windows say, "Don't buy foreign goods. Keep the money in Germany!"

Clarence W. Barron

The horrors of backing such a policy by a war machine, that would impose German goods upon other countries and keep the products of those countries out of Germany, is something to contemplate; but the deepest lesson from it is in America, which has the tariffs and not even a defensive war machine.

With the Monroe Doctrine so interpreted that no European government can enforce security for its citizens or for the property of its citizens in Mexico, and with a protective tariff under which we can invite countries to send us goods for a series of years and then suddenly bar them out, the United States may be dwelling in a fool's paradise from the political, military, and economic points of view.

A united Europe cannot be expected to lay down its arms, while arms are international arbiters, until there is a better understanding of the Monroe Doctrine and European relations to Mexico.

There is only one safety for America, and that is the rule of right and of reason. Tariffs should be neighborly; life and property made secure wherever the United States extends its sphere of influence; and arbitration should take the place of all wars.

Indeed, the United States, from every standpoint, is the one nation in the world to be the promoter of peace, and to assist in its enforcement. There is no other policy for us from the standpoint of both national righteousness and national safety.

But this subject is so large that I must present it in the next and concluding chapter.

CHAPTER XVII

WHAT PEACE SHOULD MEAN

Not When but How—The Argument for War—Right over Might—National Hate as a Political Asset—The Human Pathway—Peace by International Police—The Practical Way—Is a New Age Approaching?

The endeavor in these pages has been to show from close personal research in Europe the cause and cost of this war— cost in finance and human lives,—and also the lessons that America, and particularly the United States, should derive from this greatest war.

It is not so material when this war terminates, as how it terminates. Many people, and especially those sympathetic with Germany, are looking for a drawn battle. This means a world-disaster, and no world-progress.

The British Empire is determined that this war shall mean for generations a lasting peace by the destruction of the German war machine. The Germans likewise declare that what they are fighting for is the peace of Europe. The Germans, high and low, declare that this peace has been disrupted by jealousy of German culture, German efficiency, and German success. It is difficult to understand the German logic, for wars do not lessen jealousy, envy, or race, or national hate. They only increase the jealousy and put peace further away than before, unless there is real conquest, division, and absorption.

Bismarck declared in 1867 that he was opposed to any war upon France, and that if the military party convinced him of ability to crush France and occupy Paris, he would be unalterably opposed to the attack. For, said he, one war with France is only the first of at least six, and were we victorious in all six, it would only mean ruin for Germany, and for her neighbor and best customer.

"Do you think a poor, bankrupt, starving, ragged neighbor as desirable as a healthy, solvent, fat, well-clothed one?" demanded Bismarck.

France attacked Germany in 1870 and found her well-prepared armies impregnable. Many believe that the Allies will find the German trench-defences now impregnable. I do not think the Allies will pay the price in human sacrifice to invade Germany from the west. The break-up of Germany is more likely to come from her exhaustion and the weakness of Austria, against which the pressure will be steadily increased. But what follows the war is most important. If the victorious or defeated nations are to go on arming, they will go on warring to the extent that there be left in the world no small nations and no unfortified area.

If Germany is to grow other navies, and England is still to build two for one, North and South America must in time have navies, the support of which will burden the western hemisphere and the progress of humanity. It ought to be clear that this audacious war can mean nothing unless it means tremendous progress toward universal peace; unless it means that nations are to be guided by the same principles, practices, and morality that should guide individuals.

I know all the arguments for the needfulness of war, and there is not one of them that will hold water. Wars exist for the same reason that they formerly existed with individuals, or between cities, or states,—because there was no organization regulating the relations between individuals, cities, and states. Wars exist between nations to-day because there is no organization regulating international relations.

Out of this war and its alliances must ultimately come such a regulating of international relations, or the world goes back toward bankruptcy and barbarism.

It is declared that the people of Europe have wanted this war; that the Germans wanted to expand by war; that the French have wanted to fight for Alsace-Lorraine; that the Russians must war for a water outlet; that the English have favored war for a readjustment of the European balances in power. There are many individuals who want their neighbors' goods, or redivision; there are many cities jealous of their commercial rivals; there are many states jealous of the progress of others; but all these no longer think of war as a method of readjustment, or even of redress of grievances.

Patriotism and nationality should no more be a basis of war than civic pride or family pride.

Perhaps the first error to be blotted out before a universal peace is that which arises from the German teaching that the state is a distinct entity or individuality apart from ourselves; that a state has no moral status, no moral principles, and can do no wrong; that while we may not steal individually, we will justify ourselves in stealing, murdering, and plundering collectively, in the name of the state.

When once this error is clearly seen and rooted out, we shall still find in every community men who believe that what a man is able to get and hold is his by right of possession and power; and we shall still have police regulations, departments of justice, and courts of law, to defend the weak against injustice from the strong.

We have constitutions in civilized communities to prevent robbery and the injustice of majorities upon minorities. We have sheriffs, police, and military power to enforce the edict of right, when once the highest tribunal has made the nearest possible human approach to justice.

A distinguished lawyer once said to me that, to him, the most wonderful thing in the world was an edict of the Supreme Court of the United States; "A few words scrawled upon a scrap of paper and approved by some aged individuals of no great physical vigor; and, behold, it is instantly the law of a hundred million people!"

And, for the benefit of future human progress, the argument supporting that edict is later printed with it; and that in future any errors therein may be corrected, the wisdom of the minority or dissenting judges is as carefully preserved and bound up with the major opinion and edict, that all public sources for correction of error may be preserved in the clear amber of legal justice in truth as betwixt man and man.

> "For what avail the plow or sail,
> Or land or life, if freedom fail?"

And freedom fails when justice falls and right of might succeeds.

The breaking up of the world's physical body, or of the material dwellings and possessions of humanity, may be necessary for "a new birth of freedom"; for the incoming of the larger light; for a broader, more universal brotherhood.

Individual robbery or wrong may beget individual hate, but law in social organization prevents its full expression. The extent to which individual hate may be expanded indefinitely where guns take the place of law, may be illustrated by some communities in sparsely settled mountainous countries in our Southern states. Here family feuds and individual murder went on through generations, until nobody could tell how or why they ever began.

A journalist friend just arrived from Berlin in this month of February tells me he detects a general policy in Germany to direct the national spirit solely against England, possibly with a view to bringing the German people into line for proposals of peace with everybody else. The sentiment of Germany is being swung to-day, just as it has been from the beginning under the present Kaiser, against England as the real and only enemy to a German world-conquest.

Punch says the Germans spell "culture" with a K because England has command of all the "C's." But the English-speaking race has also command of the biggest letter in the alphabet, and can say damn with a force surpassing expression in any other language. The most popular song to-day in Germany is the "Hymn of Hate," by Ernest Lissauer, whom, it is reported, the Kaiser has decorated for this—the only real German literature from the war. It is a hymn and chant, and has rhythm, hiss, and fight in it. It runs to the sentiment,—

"French and Russian, they matter not,
A blow for a blow, a shot for a shot,"

but ends,—

"We love as one, we hate as one;
We have one foe, and one alone—

ENGLAND!"

And when that last line and that last word burst from thousands of German throats, as in the crowded cafes of Berlin, it is the fullest German damn that can find expression in German consonants. I believe the Prussians of Berlin would be as pleased to megaphone that line from Calais to Dover as they would be to throw their first shell across the English Channel. But if enforced international law did not permit them to strive for that shot as the expression of their passion, they would soon forget their hot hate and put their shoulder again beneath the progress of the world.

Man has come up from the dug-out or the cave where in primordial condition he won his food by his own hands from the uncut forests and the unfarmed waters. As family policeman he had no incentive to accumulations of food, clothing, or luxuries. These involved added police responsibilities and enlarged the temptations of his neighbors, both men and animals.

Later, his family becomes a tribe. In combination the duties of protection for the common good take on a larger view. The village, the walled city and the armed state naturally follow. Each stage of communal growth reduces the number of men set apart for defence or police duty. There is a corresponding increase in the common store of human possessions and human happinesses.

From states grow nations, then empires, until but a small fraction of the people is engaged in any way in aggressive or defensive warfare, or even police work or the determination or enforcement of laws of justice as between individuals, cities, states, or communities of any sort.

The individual club at the mouth of the cave protecting the family has become for England a surrounding line of steel ships; for the United States, of 100,000,000 people, a mere outline of a military defensive organization, to be filled in when needed. But for a few communities in the world that individual club has become a national armory, with human energies perfecting the most destructive machinery of warfare, that aggression may be carried on against neighbors, and territory expanded for purposes of national government and the increment of national wealth.

The twentieth century has been distinguished by a call to the humanities; a summons to a larger brotherhood. This has been the meaning of the clashes of the classes within all growing nations—Germany, Russia, the United States. All that outcry of humanity against mere commercialism, against the mere financial exploitation of man and his labor, in this age takes on a larger meaning.

In great wars material things go back; but the man goes to the front; and the victorious survivors make a newer and broader human creation—a new world with a new spirit.

The world has been seeking a solution of many social problems. They instantly disappear as dissolved in the hot cauldron of war. In the settlement of peace following, they are found precipitated in the fired solution, refined, clarified,—"settled."

To-day all social problems are merged in the greater problem of national existence. Alliances and a larger nationality become necessities. Man comes forth in a larger citizenship—a citizen of the whole world. There is, there can be, no other solution, no other universal peace. From this war must follow a world federation and international citizenship.

The first recognition of the brotherhood of nations may arise under the Monroe Doctrine. While this doctrine primarily is one for our national defense, it should properly embrace the defense of both North and South America, any aggression from the other side of the ocean to be unitedly resented on this side.

The increasing responsibility of nations for their fellow nations may be illustrated by the case of Cuba. The United States heard the cry of the Cubans under Spanish rule, turned out the Spanish rulers, and gave Cuba over to the Cubans. In the same spirit the United States, finding itself in possession of the Philippines, is now attempting to develop them not for the United States but for the Filipinos.

Lastly, we have the example of President Wilson, who has decreed that government by assassination in the countries to the south of us must cease, and that the United States will not recognize any government thus set up in Mexico.

It is, however, not yet incumbent upon any nation, as upon individuals, to say to its neighbor, "You shall not arm; you shall not build a war machine of aggression; your offense against one is an offense against all; your military invasion against one for purposes of expansion or self-aggrandizement will be resented by all."

Until we have practical application of a world-wide police in maintenance of the peace of nations, not alone by international agreement, which can be broken, but by agreement and international police-enforcement, so that it cannot be broken, there can be no universal peace.

We are now approaching that time.

There is no more reason why aggregations of people should have the right of murder, destruction, piracy, and pillage, than that individuals should have such right.

This is just a simple, practical question in human advancement. The world should now be big enough to grasp and effectively deal with it. The true meaning of this war is, therefore, human progress: humanity taking on larger responsibilities—the whole world answering the question, "Am I my brother's keeper?" with a thunderous, "Aye! we are one and all our brother's keeper, and we may well keep the peace of the world!"

There is no question, national or international, no question of the individual or collection of individuals, which cannot be settled by the laws which belong in the human heart. Such laws may be called spiritual or natural, divine or human; they are one and the same.

Moses wrote no new law on the tables of stone on Mount Sinai. The laws were before the tables of stone, and before the creation of the mountain itself. It was only for the people to hear and to do.

It is the same to-day. The laws of brotherhood—brotherhood of individuals, brotherhood of nations, or aggregations of individuals—are unchanged and unchangeable. It is only for the world to hear and to do.

The doctrine that war is a biological necessity must go by the board. The teaching that war is needed to harden men and nations must be placed in the realm of pagan fiction.

If war is a necessity for man, it is a necessity for woman. If it is good for men, it is good for children. If it is good for nations, it is good for states. If it is good for states, it is certainly good for cities. If it is good for peoples, it is good for individuals.

War is Hell, and from Hell. Hell may not be abolished, but it may be regulated.

Wars may not be abolished from the human heart, but they may be restrained from breaking forth to the destruction of the innocent and the guiltless.

There is only one practical way to do this, and that is to have nations under restraint, just as nations have states and cities under restraint. Then international courts of justice may perform the same work national courts now perform in respect to differences between states.

Man has come up from the individual, or dual, unit through family and tribal relation, the walled city, the policed state, into the armed nation. He is now steadily stepping forth into the world as ruler of himself, the creator of his own government, the heir and sovereign of the world. He can step into the kingdom of manhood suffrage or government only so far as the rights of his fellow men are recognized. Evil holds its own destruction, and nations that live by the sword perish by the sword.

For the United States to rush into the maelstrom of war, with organization of armies and the building of armaments, is to invite its own destruction.

For just one hundred years the North American continent has held the practical example of the impotency of the war-spirit where there is no war machinery.

By the Bush memorandum of agreement one hundred years ago it was provided that there should be no guns, forts, or naval ships on the greatest national boundary line of the world—4000 miles across the American continent between the United States and Canada. Nowhere else in the world have armed men attempted invasion, and yet provoked no war, no reprisal. What might have been the relations between the United States and Canada when the "Fenians" armed in New England and attempted a raid across the border, if there had been armies and fortifications on that border?

How securely now dwells in Canada $100,000,000 of the Bank of England reserve gold! When German representatives in the United States talk of Germany's right to invade Canada and get that gold. Uncle Sam only smiles and frowns. And the smile and the frown are potential. That boundary has been consecrated to peace; and what would be thought of the proposal, did Germany command the seas, that Uncle Sam accept some money or promises to pay and permit the German armies to go through, according to the proposal to Belgium?

In an age which has abolished human slavery, broken the walls of China, which is bringing the yellow races into the labor and white light of civilization, which has made Germany a nation, and spanned a continent with the human voice so that Boston talks with San Francisco, is it too much to expect that it can bring the boon of an international civilization, abolishing national wars?

Indeed, it is right at our doors if the United States would only welcome it and join it, instead of preparing to invite the old-world barbarism of national warfare by planning military defenses and naval fleets.

Did anybody ever hear before of ten nations, and nearly a billion people, at war, and all declaring that they are warring for purposes of peace; and may there not yet be that universal peace by reason of this war, and the war's *alliances*?

Suppose that, either before or after the nations of Europe lay down their arms, universal disarmament is assented to, and the peace of the world is entrusted to an international tribunal, which takes such part of the armies and navies as it may need to enforce its decrees, the balance so far as not needed for local police duty to be put back into industry or laid on the shelf, and all border fortifications ordered dismantled or turned into public recreation grounds—is it too much to expect in this Age?

What would be simpler than, in the end, to find fortified Heligoland, not back in the hands of England, but the naval base of a Hague Tribunal enforcing international peace?

Choose from Thousands of 1stWorldLibrary Classics By

A. M. Barnard
Ada Leverson
Adolphus William Ward
Aesop
Agatha Christie
Alexander Aaronsohn
Alexander Kielland
Alexandre Dumas
Alfred Gatty
Alfred Ollivant
Alice Duer Miller
Alice Turner Curtis
Alice Dunbar
Allen Chapman
Alleyne Ireland
Ambrose Bierce
Amelia E. Barr
Amory H. Bradford
Andrew Lang
Andrew McFarland Davis
Andy Adams
Angela Brazil
Anna Alice Chapin
Anna Sewell
Annie Besant
Annie Hamilton Donnell
Annie Payson Call
Annie Roe Carr
Annonaymous
Anton Chekhov
Archibald Lee Fletcher
Arnold Bennett
Arthur C. Benson
Arthur Conan Doyle
Arthur M. Winfield
Arthur Ransome
Arthur Schnitzler
Arthur Train
Atticus
B.H. Baden-Powell
B. M. Bower
B. C. Chatterjee
Baroness Emmuska Orczy
Baroness Orczy
Basil King
Bayard Taylor
Ben Macomber
Bertha Muzzy Bower
Bjornstjerne Bjornson

Booth Tarkington
Boyd Cable
Bram Stoker
C. Collodi
C. E. Orr
C. M. Ingleby
Carolyn Wells
Catherine Parr Traill
Charles A. Eastman
Charles Amory Beach
Charles Dickens
Charles Dudley Warner
Charles Farrar Browne
Charles Ives
Charles Kingsley
Charles Klein
Charles Hanson Towne
Charles Lathrop Pack
Charles Romyn Dake
Charles Whibley
Charles Willing Beale
Charlotte M. Braeme
Charlotte M. Yonge
Charlotte Perkins Stetson
Clair W. Hayes
Clarence Day Jr.
Clarence E. Mulford
Clemence Housman
Confucius
Coningsby Dawson
Cornelis DeWitt Wilcox
Cyril Burleigh
D. H. Lawrence
Daniel Defoe
David Garnett
Dinah Craik
Don Carlos Janes
Donald Keyhoe
Dorothy Kilner
Dougan Clark
Douglas Fairbanks
E. Nesbit
E. P. Roe
E. Phillips Oppenheim
E. S. Brooks
Earl Barnes
Edgar Rice Burroughs
Edith Van Dyne
Edith Wharton

Edward Everett Hale
Edward J. O'Biren
Edward S. Ellis
Edwin L. Arnold
Eleanor Atkins
Eleanor Hallowell Abbott
Eliot Gregory
Elizabeth Gaskell
Elizabeth McCracken
Elizabeth Von Arnim
Ellem Key
Emerson Hough
Emilie F. Carlen
Emily Bronte
Emily Dickinson
Enid Bagnold
Enilor Macartney Lane
Erasmus W. Jones
Ernie Howard Pie
Ethel May Dell
Ethel Turner
Ethel Watts Mumford
Eugene Sue
Eugenie Foa
Eugene Wood
Eustace Hale Ball
Evelyn Everett-green
Everard Cotes
F. H. Cheley
F. J. Cross
F. Marion Crawford
Fannie E. Newberry
Federick Austin Ogg
Ferdinand Ossendowski
Fergus Hume
Florence A. Kilpatrick
Fremont B. Deering
Francis Bacon
Francis Darwin
Frances Hodgson Burnett
Frances Parkinson Keyes
Frank Gee Patchin
Frank Harris
Frank Jewett Mather
Frank L. Packard
Frank V. Webster
Frederic Stewart Isham
Frederick Trevor Hill
Frederick Winslow Taylor

Friedrich Kerst	Hayden Carruth	James Branch Cabell
Friedrich Nietzsche	Helent Hunt Jackson	James DeMille
Fyodor Dostoyevsky	Helen Nicolay	James Joyce
G.A. Henty	Hendrik Conscience	James Lane Allen
G.K. Chesterton	Hendy David Thoreau	James Lane Allen
Gabrielle E. Jackson	Henri Barbusse	James Oliver Curwood
Garrett P. Serviss	Henrik Ibsen	James Oppenheim
Gaston Leroux	Henry Adams	James Otis
George A. Warren	Henry Ford	James R. Driscoll
George Ade	Henry Frost	Jane Abbott
Geroge Bernard Shaw	Henry James	Jane Austen
George Cary Eggleston	Henry Jones Ford	Jane L. Stewart
George Durston	Henry Seton Merriman	Janet Aldridge
George Ebers	Henry W Longfellow	Jens Peter Jacobsen
George Eliot	Herbert A. Giles	Jerome K. Jerome
George Gissing	Herbert Carter	Jessie Graham Flower
George MacDonald	Herbert N. Casson	John Buchan
George Meredith	Herman Hesse	John Burroughs
George Orwell	Hildegard G. Frey	John Cournos
George Sylvester Viereck	Homer	John F. Kennedy
George Tucker	Honore De Balzac	John Gay
George W. Cable	Horace B. Day	John Glasworthy
George Wharton James	Horace Walpole	John Habberton
Gertrude Atherton	Horatio Alger Jr.	John Joy Bell
Gordon Casserly	Howard Pyle	John Kendrick Bangs
Grace E. King	Howard R. Garis	John Milton
Grace Gallatin	Hugh Lofting	John Philip Sousa
Grace Greenwood	Hugh Walpole	John Taintor Foote
Grant Allen	Humphry Ward	Jonas Lauritz Idemil Lie
Guillermo A. Sherwell	Ian Maclaren	Jonathan Swift
Gulielma Zollinger	Inez Haynes Gillmore	Joseph A. Altsheler
Gustav Flaubert	Irving Bacheller	Joseph Carey
H. A. Cody	Isabel Cecilia Williams	Joseph Conrad
H. B. Irving	Isabel Hornibrook	Joseph E. Badger Jr
H.C. Bailey	Israel Abrahams	Joseph Hergesheimer
H. G. Wells	Ivan Turgenev	Joseph Jacobs
H. H. Munro	J.G.Austin	Jules Vernes
H. Irving Hancock	J. Henri Fabre	Julian Hawthrone
H. R. Naylor	J. M. Barrie	Julie A Lippmann
H. Rider Haggard	J. M. Walsh	Justin Huntly McCarthy
H. W. C. Davis	J. Macdonald Oxley	Kakuzo Okakura
Haldeman Julius	J. R. Miller	Karle Wilson Baker
Hall Caine	J. S. Fletcher	Kate Chopin
Hamilton Wright Mabie	J. S. Knowles	Kenneth Grahame
Hans Christian Andersen	J. Storer Clouston	Kenneth McGaffey
Harold Avery	J. W. Duffield	Kate Langley Bosher
Harold McGrath	Jack London	Kate Langley Bosher
Harriet Beecher Stowe	Jacob Abbott	Katherine Cecil Thurston
Harry Castlemon	James Allen	Katherine Stokes
Harry Coghill	James Andrews	L. A. Abbot
Harry Houidini	James Baldwin	L. T. Meade

L. Frank Baum	Owen Johnson	Stephen Crane
Latta Griswold	P.G. Wodehouse	Stewart Edward White
Laura Dent Crane	Paul and Mabel Thorne	Stijn Streuvels
Laura Lee Hope	Paul G. Tomlinson	Swami Abhedananda
Laurence Housman	Paul Severing	Swami Parmananda
Lawrence Beasley	Percy Brebner	T. S. Ackland
Leo Tolstoy	Percy Keese Fitzhugh	T. S. Arthur
Leonid Andreyev	Peter B. Kyne	The Princess Der Ling
Lewis Carroll	Plato	Thomas A. Janvier
Lewis Sperry Chafer	Quincy Allen	Thomas A Kempis
Lilian Bell	R. Derby Holmes	Thomas Anderton
Lloyd Osbourne	R. L. Stevenson	Thomas Bailey Aldrich
Louis Hughes	R. S. Ball	Thomas Bulfinch
Louis Joseph Vance	Rabindranath Tagore	Thomas De Quincey
Louis Tracy	Rahul Alvares	Thomas Dixon
Louisa May Alcott	Ralph Bonehill	Thomas H. Huxley
Lucy Fitch Perkins	Ralph Henry Barbour	Thomas Hardy
Lucy Maud Montgomery	Ralph Victor	Thomas More
Luther Benson	Ralph Waldo Emmerson	Thornton W. Burgess
Lydia Miller Middleton	Rene Descartes	U. S. Grant
Lyndon Orr	Ray Cummings	Upton Sinclair
M. Corvus	Rex Beach	Valentine Williams
M. H. Adams	Rex E. Beach	Various Authors
Margaret E. Sangster	Richard Harding Davis	Vaughan Kester
Margret Howrh	Richard Jefferies	Victor Appleton
Margaret Vandercook	Richard Le Gallienne	Victor G. Durham
Margaret W. Hungerford	Robert Barr	Victoria Cross
Margret Penrose	Robert Frost	Virginia Woolf
Maria Edgeworth	Robert Gordon Anderson	Wadsworth Camp
Maria Thompson Daviess	Robert L. Drake	Walter Camp
Mariano Azuela	Robert Lansing	Walter Scott
Marion Polk Angellotti	Robert Lynd	Washington Irving
Mark Overton	Robert Michael Ballantyne	Wilbur Lawton
Mark Twain	Robert W. Chambers	Wilkie Collins
Mary Austin	Rosa Nouchette Carey	Willa Cather
Mary Catherine Crowley	Rudyard Kipling	Willard F. Baker
Mary Cole	Saint Augustine	William Dean Howells
Mary Hastings Bradley	Samuel B. Allison	William le Queux
Mary Roberts Rinehart	Samuel Hopkins Adams	W. Makepeace Thackeray
Mary Rowlandson	Sarah Bernhardt	William W. Walter
M. Wollstonecraft Shelley	Sarah C. Hallowell	William Shakespeare
Maud Lindsay	Selma Lagerlof	Winston Churchill
Max Beerbohm	Sherwood Anderson	Yei Theodora Ozaki
Myra Kelly	Sigmund Freud	Yogi Ramacharaka
Nathaniel Hawthrone	Standish O'Grady	Young E. Allison
Nicolo Machiavelli	Stanley Weyman	Zane Grey
O. F. Walton	Stella Benson	
Oscar Wilde	Stella M. Francis	